THE WORD'S WAY

THE WORD'S WAY

Volume III
Studies in Abundant Living

Victor Paul Wierwille

American Christian Press
The Way International
New Knoxville, Ohio 45871

Other books by Victor Paul Wierwille

Power for Abundant Living
Receiving The Holy Spirit Today
Are The Dead Alive Now
The Bible Tells Me So
  Volume I, Studies in Abundant Living
The New, Dynamic Church
  Volume II, Studies in Abundant Living

Standard Book Number ISBN 0-910068-04-6
Library of Congress Catalog Card Number 70-176281
American Christian Press
The Way International
New Knoxville, Ohio 45871
Published 1973
Printed in the United States of America

iv

To my daughter
Sara Kathryn Wierwille

Contents

Preface   ix

Part I   The Law and Order of God   1

  1. *In the Beginning*   3
  2. *Who Is the Word?*   25
  3. *Body, Soul, Spirit*   45
  4. *The Unforgivable Sin*   57
  5. *Sons of God: Adoption and Birth*   71
  6. *The Third Heaven and Earth*   87

Part II Points of View   107

  7. *Viewpoints: God's—Man's*   109
  8. *Of Human Sacrifice*   131

Part III The Credentials of Jesus Christ   143

  9. *The Genealogy of Jesus Christ*   145
 10. *The Conception of Jesus Christ*   157
 11. *The Lord's Brethren*   175

Part IV Jesus Christ the End of the Law   185

 12. *The Day Jesus Christ Died*   187
 13. *Did Jesus Keep the Passover?*   201

14. Simon of Cyrene and
    the Cross Christ Bore   219
15. The Four Crucified With Jesus   235
16. The Burial of Jesus   249
17. The Cry of Triumph   267

About the Author   275

Preface

The Word's Way is organized into four parts: "The Law and Order of God," "Points of View," "The Credentials of Jesus Christ" and "Jesus Christ the End of the Law." Within each part are chapters, each chapter having been researched and originally written as an individual study. By loosely grouping the studies into general topics, a person can get a broader perspective as the parts fit together to make up the larger whole.

However, because the chapters were written as individual studies and then put into topical units, occasionally a reader may find that all facets of the topic are not covered. This problem will be solved as more exhaustive research and writing are completed. In the meantime, I know the contents of Volume III of "Studies in Abundant Living" will not only open up more of God's Word for you, but will also lift you — mentally and physically and spiritually.

Let us put God's Word in our hearts and minds for it alone can give us complete deliverance from the darkness of this world.

Part I

The Law and
Order of God

Part I

The Law and Order of God

When God formed, made and created the universe, He saw to its orderliness. The universe was not thrown together haphazardly. Within this orderly sphere laws were imposed to maintain that order and to insure justice.

Now if we are ever going to understand God's laws and His order, we must have a knowledge of the beginning of the universe. This we find in its thrilling clarity in the first and second chapters of Genesis, as studied in "In the Beginning."

"Who Is The Word?" delves into the Word of God for a basic research of the relationship of God, His Word, His Son and the Holy Spirit. The critical verse of study is John 1:1 which, when rightly divided, crystalizes a very important key to understanding The Word.

God, in bringing about man, made man a three-part

1

being. Genesis shows the significance of each part in nature and in animal life. Only after "Body, Soul, Spirit" is understood can a person grasp what happens when a person commits the sin against the Holy Spirit, also called "The Unforgivable Sin."

Throughout The Word we read of God's having sons — His earthly children who believe on Him. But in the order and laws set up by God, God could not have sons with His seed in them until Christ had regained what Adam gave away. "Sons of God: Adoption and Birth" goes into the laws by which God abided so that God could have sons by birth instead of by adoption.

"The Third Heaven and Earth" is the final chapter in "The Law and Order of God." This sets the overall universal time line. The Bible speaks of three heavens and earths; and Biblical research pinpoints the timing of each and why, in the course of the universe, there needs to be three.

This Part I on "The Law and Order of God" is very important; it is crucial and sharply accurate in giving an understanding of the larger picture of life. So when you finish reading this section, go back and carefully study each chapter again. You will thrill at God's order and how He Himself works within the game plan of His law.

CHAPTER ONE

In The Beginning

"In the beginning God created the heaven and the earth."

Genesis 1:1 properly reads, "God created the heavens and the earth in the beginning." Placing "God" first in the verse and in the Word of God puts Him in His proper position.

The words "in the beginning," *breashith* in Hebrew, mean "origin" or *genēsis* in Greek. The word "God," *Elohim,* is plural to emphasize God's creative greatness. "Heaven," *shamayim,* also is in the plural form to point out the vastness of this expanse. The heavens are so extensive that even though man has reached the moon, he has not begun to explore the heavens which God created in the beginning.

Verse 1 sets like a diamond. If I had divided the Bible into chapters, I would have made this one verse a chapter in itself and started chapter 2 with what now is verse 2 of chapter 1. The reason for my dividing the first part of Genesis into chapters in this way is that trillions of years may have elapsed between verse 1 and verse 2. No one knows the length of time between the events recorded in verses 1 and 2; but it is known that when the account given by verse 2 begins, something catastrophic had happened in the heavens and on the earth. In the beginning when God created the heavens and the earth, all the creation was in perfect condition. But an astounding change occurred by the time of the record of Genesis 1:2. About this cataclysmic occurrence, II Peter 3 gives more information.

II Peter 3:5—7:
For this they willingly are ignorant of, that by the word of God the heavens were of old, and the earth standing out of the water and in the water:

Whereby the world that then was, being overflowed with water, perished·

But the heavens and the earth, which are now, by the same word are kept in store, reserved unto fire against the day of judgment and perdition of ungodly men.

II Peter states that there were the original heavens and earth of Genesis 1:1, and then came the heavens and earth which are now. This present heavens and earth are the ones which will last unti the judgment. But, after the judgment, II Peter records that there will be the third heaven and earth.

II Peter 3:13:
... look for new heavens and a new earth, wherein dwelleth righteousness.

A further corroboration of II Peter 3:13 is given in Revelation.

Revelation 21:1:
And I saw a new heaven and a new earth: for the first [former] heaven and the first [former] earth were passed away; and there wa. no more sea.*

Thus the Bible designates three periods of time in referring to heaven and earth. The first one is Genesis 1:1, the second one follows Genesis 1:2 until the time of the "last judgment," which occasion ushers in the third heaven and earth. The heavens and earth which are now, the second heavens and earth, begin with Genesis 1:3, and their formation is completed

*See Chapter 6, "The Third Heaven and Earth."

when Genesis 2:1 says, "Thus the heavens and the earth were finished ...."

The last three words of Genesis 1:1 are "and the earth." Immediately following, verse 2 begins with the same phrase, "And the earth ...." This is a figure of speech called *anadiplosis*, meaning that the next thought begins with the same words ending the previous thought, a repetition. Within this figure of speech is another figure: the repeated usage of the word "and." In the "original" text, the first word in the Bible would be "God." But the rest of the verses in chapter 1 begin with the word "and." This figure of speech is called *polysyndeton*. There are 102 separate acts of God listed in the 34 verses following Genesis 1:1, and all the acts begin with "and." The purpose of this figure of speech is to emphasize God throughout: "God created, and God ..., and God ..., and God ...." God was always the prime mover. These "ands" are used with divine design, not haphazardly.

When God created the heavens and the earth in the beginning, He did not create them in the chaos found in verse 2.

> Genesis 1:2:
> And the earth was without form, and void; and darkness *was* upon the face of the deep. And the Spirit of God moved upon the face of the waters.

First of all, in examining verse 2 a student of The Word must be aware that in the original Estrangelo Aramaic and Hebrew there was no verb "to be," although there was the verb "to become." This is the reason the first "was" in verse 2 is in regular print while the second "was" is italicized. It points out that there was no Hebrew word in the second usage; there was no word at that place at all, but there was a word for the first usage. The first word "was" should have been translated "became." "And the earth became without form and void ...." The earth was not created in Genesis 1:1 formless and void, but it became that way.

The words "form, and void" are a figure of speech, *paronomasia,* meaning "similar in sound but not in sense or meaning." One does not understand this by reading the English words "form, and void," for they do not have similar sounds. But the Hebrew words, *tohu va bohu,* are similar in sound but not in meaning.

Isaiah 45 and Jeremiah 4 point out that the heavens and earth were not created *tohu va bohu.*

Isaiah 45:18:
For thus saith the Lord that created the heavens; God himself that formed the earth and made it; he hath established it, he created it not in vain [*tohu*] ....

7

> Jeremiah 4:23:
> I beheld the earth, and, lo, *it was* without form,
> and void [*tohu va bohu*] ....

God did not create the heavens and the earth *tohu va bohu,* the condition in which it was found in Genesis 1:2. The whole creation was originally perfect. Isaiah tells more about how the earth became without form and void. Isaiah records that in the beginning, sometime before Genesis 1:2, God created angels, spirit beings. When He created these angels, He put all the angels under three heads: Gabriel, Michael and Lucifer. But celestial strife ensued, with Lucifer and a third of the angels trying to usurp the throne of God. Consequently these spirit beings were dispelled from heaven and became known as the fallen angels, the enemies of God.

Ezekiel 28 speaks of Lucifer who was at one time the angel of light.

> Ezekiel 28:15:
> Thou [Lucifer] *wast* perfect in thy ways from
> the day that thou wast created, till iniquity was
> found in thee.

Whatever happened between Genesis 1:1 and 1:2 was of such a cataclysmic nature that a perfectly created earth became *tohu va bohu.* When Lucifer rebelled in heaven, the whole creation rocked and reeled. Romans 8 says that even until today the "whole creation groaneth and travaileth in pain ...."

Genesis 1:2 begins the record of God's putting His creation in order after the first heaven and earth.

Genesis 1:2:
And the earth was [became] without form, and void; and darkness *was* upon the face of the deep. And the Spirit of God moved upon the face of the waters.

"And the Spirit of God moved upon the face of the waters." The word "moved" is also the word "brooded." The Spirit of God is pictured as a hen brooding, sitting on eggs. This is a figure of speech, *anthropopatheia* or *condescensio,* where God is given attributes of animal life. What is God going to hatch? He is going to bring into existence the earth as we know it today. Figuratively, God was sitting on a situation which was ready to crack out like the chick bursts out of the egg shell. What does God bring about after His brooding? The third verse begins giving the record.

Genesis 1:3:
And God said, Let there be light: and there was light.

Why did God not have to *create* light? Because whatever light is composed of already existed. God had created it in the beginning, and now it simply needed to be put together. The next question people frequently have when they read verse 3 is: "What specifically happened when Genesis records 'And God said'?" "And God said" is all the Word of God tells us. A person cannot know more than The Word tells. There undoubtedly are numerous things we would like to know, but remember the knowledge given to us in Deuteronomy 29:29: "The secret *things belong* unto the Lord our God: but those *things which are* revealed *belong* unto us and to our children for ever, that *we* may do all the words of this law." Verse 5 of Genesis says, "And God called ...." Verse 6 records, "And God said ...." Verse 9 reports, "And God said ...." All we know is that when God spoke, what He spoke came to pass.

Verse 3 of Genesis 1 and the rest of chapter 1 into chapter 2 relate the events of God's putting this earth back in order so that it was habitable for one of the greatest things God was going to do: the forming, the making and the creating of man.

Verses 4 and 5 explain what happened after God spoke light into existence.

Genesis 1:4,5:
And God saw the light, that *it was* good: and

God divided the light from the darkness.

And God called the light Day, and the darkness he called Night. And the evening and the morning were the first day.

The "evening and the morning" is a figure of speech called *synecdoche,* meaning that the beginning and the ending stand for the entire period. Evening and morning are meant to represent the entire day, a period of twenty-four hours.

Genesis 1:6–8:
And God said, Let there be a firmament in the midst of the waters, and let it divide the waters from the waters.

And God made the firmament, and divided the waters which *were* under the firmament from the waters which *were* above the firmament: and it was so.

And God called the firmament Heaven. And the evening and the morning were the second day.

The word "firmament" throughout this passage is "expanse." "And God called the expanse heaven," meaning "lofty" or "high." Biblically speaking, any place above the earth is heaven. Whenever anything is not in contact with the earth, it is in heaven.

Genesis 1:9,10:
And God said, Let the waters under the heaven
be gathered together unto one place, and let the
dry *land* appear: and it was so.

And God called the dry *land* Earth; and the
gathering together of the waters called he Seas:
and God saw that *it was* good.

In the first nine verses of Genesis 1, the word
"earth" refers to the planet; beginning with verse 9,
"earth" refers to dry land.

Genesis 1:11:
And God said, Let the earth [dry land] bring
forth grass, the herb yielding seed, *and* the fruit
tree yielding fruit after his kind, whose seed *is* in
itself, upon the earth: and it was so.

Verse 11 divulges many interesting truths. First,
note that it says all are to bring forth after their kind.
"Kind" is the word *genos* in the Septuagint, transliterated into English as "genus." This means that
when a cow is bred to a bull, a calf will be the result,
not a lamb. A dog and a cow cannot breed and get a
cow-dog, nor will a cat and a dog produce a catty-dog
or a doggy-cat. Why? Because everything comes after
its kind, after its genus. There can be evolution or
change within a genus but not between genera.

Variety occurs within a genus. For example, there are big cows and small cows, black, red and white cows; there are Guernseys, Jerseys and Brown Swiss. Much variety has occurred within the bovine genus, but this genus has not crossed with another genus, or Genesis 1:11 would not be true.

An example of not accurately following the teaching of The Word regarding everything "after its kind" is found in an interpretation of Genesis 6.*

Genesis 6:1—4:

And it came to pass, when men began to multiply on the face of the earth, and daughters were born unto them.

That the sons of God saw the daughters of men that they *were* fair; and they took them wives of all which they chose.

And the Lord said, My spirit shall not always strive with man, for that he also *is* flesh: yet his days shall be an hundred and twenty years.

There were giants in the earth in those days; and also after that, when the sons of God came in unto the daughters of men, and they bare *children* to them, the same *became* mighty men which *were* of old, men of renown.

*"His" in "after his kind" is "its." There is no neuter form in Estrangelo Aramaic nor in Hebrew.

The Law and Order of God

Some teach that wicked angels cohabited with human beings. These teachers propound that the offspring of these angels and human beings were the giants,* *nephilim,* which infiltrated mankind and which were responsible for bringing about the destruction of all mankind with the exception of Noah, his wife, three sons and their wives. This teaching is not Biblically accurate. If angels, who are spirit beings, can cohabit with a human, then genera have interbred. Cohabitation of angels with man cannot be possible, for the Bible says that each produces after its kind. In context Genesis 6:4 refers to the faithful of God as "the sons of God" and those unbelieving persons as "daughters of men," regardless of whether male or female. When believers wandered from their own and married unbelievers, trouble ensued. Of course, the offspring of these marriages were products of parents of the same genus. No problem exists in Genesis 6 if readers don't make one.

Everything must be after its kind "whose seed *is* in itself." Seed, the potential for offspring, is "in itself." All life is passed on through seed, whether the life be plant or animal. In animal life seed comes from the male. When the sperm of the male, which contains

---

*They were giants or champions of wickedness. The root of the Hebrew word *nephilim* means "to fall." They were "fallen ones." The Estrangelo Aramaic gives this word as the intensive form of *gbra*, meaning "very mighty men or champions." The word "giants," *gigantes,* was used in the Septuagint, the Syriac Version and the Vulgate.

14

the seed for the new life, impregnates the female egg, a new life begins. In animals the soul-life is in the blood, as Leviticus 17:11 records, "The life of the flesh *is* in the blood."

Since all men come from the same blood, the question arises as to how the blood was carried along after the first generation on earth — Adam and Eve's children. In other words, whom did the children of Adam and Eve marry? The only persons available for the sons and daughters of Adam and Eve were each other. Cain married his sister, as did Abel, Seth and the other children. In our day the bloodlines have become so contaminated that intra-family marriage is forbidden by law as too many undesirable characteristics come out with close in-breeding of humans. But Adam's children could only marry each other.

The sons of Adam married their own sisters. If we had pure bloodstreams, we could marry our sisters. The reason we are not allowed now to marry sisters is that the impurities in our blood would cause complications in the following generations.

Because of purer blood, people lived longer as the early Biblical records tell. Some people try to explain early man's longevity by saying that their years weren't as long as ours; but that simply isn't true.

Time then was the same as now. The reason for such longevity was that their blood had not become so contaminated, so impure. Marriage and sin eventually began to produce weaker people who, therefore, died at an earlier age.

The words "seed in itself" are the figure of speech *polyptoton,* meaning the same part of speech but with a different inflection. To literalize verse 11, it would read "... after its kind seeding seed upon the earth: and it was so."

> Genesis 1:12–26:
> And the earth brought forth grass, *and* herb yielding seed after his kind, and the tree yielding fruit, whose seed *was* in itself, after his kind: and God saw that *it was* good.
>
> And the evening and the morning were the third day.
>
> And God said, Let there be lights in the firmament of the heaven to divide the day from the night; and let them be for signs, and for seasons, and for days, and years:
>
> And let them be for lights in the firmament of the heaven to give light upon the earth: and it was so.

And God made two great lights; the greater light to rule the day, and the lesser light to rule the night: *he made* the stars also.

And God set them in the firmament of the heaven to give light upon the earth.

And to rule over the day and over the night, and to divide the light from the darkness: and God saw that *it was* good.

And the evening and the morning were the fourth day.

And God said, Let the waters bring forth abundantly the moving creature that hath life, and fowl *that* may fly above the earth in the open firmament of heaven.

And God created great whales, and every living creature that moveth, which the waters brought forth abundantly, after their kind, and every winged fowl after his kind: and God saw that *it was* good.

And God blessed them, saying, Be fruitful, and multiply, and fill the waters in the seas, and let fowl multiply in the earth.

And the evening and the morning were the fifth day.

And God said, Let the earth bring forth the living creature after his kind, cattle, and creeping thing, and beast of the earth after his kind: and it was so.

And God made the beast of the earth after his kind, and cattle after their kind, and every thing that creepeth upon the earth after his kind: and God saw that *it was* good.

And God said, Let us make man in our image, after our likeness: and let them have dominion over the fish of the sea, and over the fowl of the air, and over the cattle, and over all the earth, and over every creeping thing that creepeth upon the earth.

Several modern theologians have conjectured that the words "Let us" in verse 26 prove that God is discussing the situation with Jesus — that is why the text reads "us," instead of, "Let me make man ...." If God were talking to Jesus, the problems of Biblical accuracy elsewhere are going to become overwhelming. This usage of "us" in verse 26 is similar to the English expression used by a monarch when the monarch refers to himself as ruler and source of authority. When speaking in her official capacity, the Queen of England to this very day uses the expression, "We, the Queen of England." When God said, "Let us make man in our image, after our likeness," He used "us" for He was speaking of Himself as supreme ruler.

"Our image after our likeness" is the figure of speech *hendiadys*, meaning "two for one" — two words used for one thing meant. God was going to make man in His own (1) image and (2) likeness. God's image and likeness is Spirit according to John 4:24.

> Genesis 1:27,28:
> So God created man in his *own* [this word was added in the translation and should be deleted] image, in the image of God created he him; male and female created he them.*
>
> And God blessed them, and God said unto them, Be fruitful, and multiply, and replenish the earth, and subdue it: and have dominion over the fish of the sea, and over the fowl of the air, and over every living thing that moveth upon the earth.

God could communicate with Adam and Eve, but not with the animals. The usage of "them" in verse

*God created both male and female, Adam and Eve, in His image, spirit.

19

27 is a figure called *prolepsis,* meaning "to know before it happens that it will happen and speaking of future things as present realities." God knew that Adam and Eve would be fruitful and that they would multiply. He further added, "... and replenish the earth." The word "replenish" brings out a very interesting point. How can one replenish the earth if life had never been there before? That is why God must have had something else going on in Genesis 1:1 besides, and in addition to, the angels which He created. There must have been beings upon the earth before the establishment of the earth as it is known today which is recorded in verse 2, because God said to Adam and Eve, "You replenish the earth." If they were going to replenish it, the earth must have been "plenished" before. In that period of time was prehistoric man.

When scientists find bones of so-called animals, including man, there is now no problem. In putting ancient bones together and concluding it to be man or another type of animal, scientists deduce that these findings represent man as he was evolving into the present day *homo sapiens.* This deduction is Biblically inaccurate. For although the anthropologists have bones to work with, they have never seen the life that mobilized those bones. Scientists assume that prehistoric life was the same type of life known in man and animals today. But this is the point at which the scientists reach the wrong conclusion. The Word says so. Soul-life, as it is presently known, was not created until Genesis 1:21 when God created it in animals. Therefore, whatever the life of the pre-historic beings was, it could *not* have been soul-life as known today. If their life had been the type of life that is in beings today, God would not have had to create it. Anthropologists' findings could not be man as we know him today, for what God called "man" was not formed, made nor created until the second earth came into being *after* Genesis 1:1.

Surely God was not limited. He could and did have some type of life in the prehistoric animals to make them mobile. Because the earth had been populated before, God could rightly say to Adam and Eve, "Replenish the earth and subdue it."

"To subdue" means "to tame it and take it over," for there was no one above Adam and Eve except God. Adam was God's steward; he ran the whole show. In the beginning God gave man rulership, dominion, authority and power over all His creation. We know this power was lost somehow because man certainly does not now have dominion, authority, rulership nor power. Even the smallest things which can barely be seen under a microscope are killing people constantly. Originally man had dominion and power, but man lost it — and not without Biblical explanation.

21

Genesis 1:29–2:2:

And God said, Behold, I have given you every herb bearing seed, which *is* upon the face of all the earth, and every tree, in the which *is* the fruit of a tree yielding seed; to you it shall be for meat.

And to every beast of the earth, and to every fowl of the air, and to every thing that creepeth upon the earth, wherein *there is* life, *I have given* every green herb for meat: and it was so.

And God saw every thing that he had made, and, behold, *it was* very good [not just good, but *very* good]. And the evening and the morning were the sixth day.

Thus the heavens and the earth were finished, and all the host of them [This is the second heavens and earth as recorded in II Peter 3:7.].

And on [by*] the seventh day God ended his work which he had made; and he rested on the seventh day from all his work which he had made.

God ended His work on the sixth day and He rested on the seventh.

God didn't rest because of fatigue; He rested from

*The word "on" in Estrangelo Aramaic is the prefix "b." In both the Estrangelo Aramaic and Hebrew this prefix may be translated "on," "by," "at" or "near" among other things. In context it is very clear that the translation should be "by."

22

His activity. It was finished. When the Bible records that Jesus Christ ascended into heaven and sat down, the same word, "rested," is used. His job was finished. Again on Pentecost, as recorded in Acts 2, the spirit sat on each of the believers; the same word, "rested," is used. When Christ, by way of the holy spirit, came into believers on and following the day of Pentecost, all the power and authority was reestablished in believers. What man had lost in power, authority, rulership and dominion since Genesis 1:28, he regains when the holy spirit comes within.

> Genesis 2:3:
> And God blessed the seventh day, and sanctified it: because that in it he had rested from all his work which God created and made.

The next twenty-three verses, from Genesis 2:4 to 25, simply give the details and amplifications of chapter 1. Genesis 2:9–14 could chronologically be inserted between verses 12 and 13 of chapter 1.

To understand how God organized this second heaven and earth and the rules which were originally established, we must have a minute and detailed knowledge of the first few chapters of Genesis. We must understand the origins of life and its laws if we are to perceive the greatness of God's Word and the justness of His laws. In Genesis lies the foundation of the accuracy of His matchless Word.

CHAPTER TWO

Who is the Word?
John 1:1–18

Since the early centuries after Christ, Christian doctrine in many instances has taught that Jesus was co-existent with God — Jesus either in spirit or in some other form was with God from the beginning. The doctrines which hold or have held this idea that God is Jesus and Jesus is God substantiate their beliefs by isolating bits of Biblical texts. Genesis 1:26 is their initial point of departure where God says, "Let us make man in our image...." "Us" and "our" are interpreted to mean God and Jesus Christ.

This Scripture is no proof of Jesus' existence in the beginning. The first person plural pronouns, "us" and "our," are used to indicate the magnitude of the incident to which God related Himself. A monarch often uses the plural pronoun when speaking of himself in his official position. For example, to this very day. Elizabeth II uses the expression "we" when speaking of herself. Elizabeth is not a "we" but yet

25

she speaks of herself in her official position in the plural. In this same grammatical sense God employs the plural pronouns. "Let us make man in our image, after our likeness ...."

The Bible teaches that there is only one true God, that God was in Christ,* that God is Spirit,† and that God is eternal whereas Jesus was born. Matthew 1:18 says, "Now the birth of Jesus Christ was on this wise ...." The word for "birth" is *genēsis, genō* meaning "beginning" and *nēsos* meaning "island, or something separate from the main body."**

The first chapter of the Gospel of John has been misread and interpreted as follows: "In the beginning was Jesus Christ, and Jesus Christ was with God, and Jesus Christ was God." This is not what the verse says.

> John 1:1:
> In the beginning was the Word, and the Word was with God, and the Word was God.

---

*II Corinthians 5:19: "To wit, that God was in Christ, reconciling the world unto himself, not imputing their trespasses unto them; and hath committed unto us the word of reconciliation."

†John 4:24: "God *is* a Spirit: and they that worship him must worship *him* in spirit and in truth."

Hebrews 9:14: "How much more shall the blood of Christ, who through the eternal Spirit offered himself without spot to God, purge your conscience from dead works to serve the living God?"

**Acts 13:6; 28:1,7,9,11.

The question of John 1:1 is: Who is "the Word" or what is "the Word." Genesis 1:1 plainly states, "In the beginning God ...." God alone was from the beginning, therefore, it is God who is "the Word" of John 1:1.

How does God who is Spirit communicate Himself as "the Word" with man who is flesh? Human beings communicate with each other by way of symbols, be they spoken words, pictures or sign language. These symbols communicate ideas and thoughts. But Spirit cannot communicate with mind, senses or reason as they are two separate and well-defined categories. Spirit and flesh are in two different realms and each one must stay within its own boundary. Spirit can communicate with spirit only, and flesh by way of its senses can communicate only with the senses or the material realm. How then does God overcome these communication barriers?

God who is Spirit manifests Himself to men in the flesh in three ways: (1) by His Spirit which was upon special people in the Old Testament and which is in those born again during our administration; (2) by His only-begotten Son, Jesus Christ; (3) by His written Word, including the spoken words of the prophets.

God, to manifest Himself in the world of the flesh,

had to use a concrete form for the senses to recognize. God gave the revealed Word so that man by his natural faculties might be able to understand the communication from God. When John 1:1 says, "... and the Word was with God," it refers to both (1) the written Word which has come to us as the Bible and (2) His created Word which is known as Jesus Christ. If in John 1:1 the word "revealed" were placed before "Word," the verse would be precise and Biblically accurate: "In the beginning was the Word [God] and the [revealed] Word was with God ...."

How was this revealed Word with God? The Word was with God in His foreknowledge. God is omniscient, knowing all things: He knew from before the foundation of the world that the formed, made and created man would sin; He knew from before the foundation of the world that Jesus Christ would redeem man; He knew from before the foundation of the world that it would be possible for man to be born again; He knows our end as well as our beginning. This is what John 1:1 literally says. The revealed Word was with God in His foreknowledge; the revealed Word was later to be manifested in writing as the Bible and in the flesh as Jesus Christ.

How was Jesus with God in the beginning? In the same way that the written Word was with Him — in God's foreknowledge. God knew that Jesus Christ would be born and that He would redeem man. From

28

the beginning Jesus Christ was with God in His fore-knowledge, as we the chosen of God were called in Him in His foreknowledge. Ephesians 1:4 says, "According as he [God] hath chosen us in him [God] before the foundation of the world ...." We were in God's foreknowledge.

God, who is Spirit, to manifest Himself in concretion, necessitated revealing Himself and His will in words and in His human Son. He revealed Himself through The Word, *logos.* God's communication of Himself as the *logos* came into manifestation when "... holy men of God spake *as they were* moved by the Holy Ghost."* And, when the fullness of time came, Jesus Christ who was God's communication of Himself in the flesh was born.†

"And the word was God" means that the written Word was as much God speaking as the words of Jesus Christ were God speaking.

John 1:2:
The same was in the beginning with God.

"The same" is this revealed Word which was with God in His foreknowledge from the very beginning. Verse 2 is a repetition of what we just noted in verse 1.

*II Peter 1:21: "For the prophecy came not in old time by the will of man: but holy men of God spake *as they were* moved by the Holy Ghost."
†John 1:14: "And the Word was made flesh, and dwelt among us, (and we beheld his glory, the glory as of the only begotten of the Father,) full of grace and truth."

Why the repetition? To establish what has been said. Whenever God doubles a statement in The Word, the absoluteness is established.* This truth concerning the revealed Word is so great, so magnificent and so wonderful, that God had it written twice just to emphasize it and to indicate the definite establishment of the truth of John 1:1.

The preposition "with" in verses 1 and 2 of John 1 further confirms this whole truth: "... and the Word was with [*pros*] God .... The same was in the beginning with [*pros*] God." There are a vast number of different Greek prepositions translated "with," but only *pros* could fit here. *Pros* means "together with and yet having distinct independence." The revealed Word was together *with* God and yet distinctly independent of Him. This removes the guessing from John 1:1 and 2 and makes it logical and in order with the laws used in language as well as with the whole Word of God.

> John 1:1, 2:
>
> In the beginning was the Word [God], and the [revealed] Word was with [*pros*] God [with Him in His foreknowledge, yet independent of Him], and the Word was God.
>
> The same [revealed Word] was in the beginning with [*pros*] God.

*Genesis 41:32: "And for that the dream was doubled unto Pharaoh twice: *it is* because the thing *is* established by God, and God will shortly bring it to pass."

Verse 2 could literally read, "The same [the written Word which is the Bible and the Word in the flesh which is Jesus Christ] was in the beginning with God [in His foreknowledge]."

The following Scriptures enable us to more fully understand God's communication to man by way of the prophets who gave us the written Word and by His Son Jesus Christ who was sent by God.

> Psalms 107:20:
> He [God] sent his word [by way of the prophets], and healed them ....

> John 5:36:
> ... the same works that I do, bear witness of me, that the Father hath sent me.

> John 5:38:
> And ye have not his word abiding in you: for whom he hath sent, him ye believe not.

> John 17:3:
> ... that they might know thee the only true God, and Jesus Christ, whom thou hast sent.

Verse 3 continues the information divulged in the first two verses of John 1.

31

John 1:3:
All things were made by him [God]; and
without him [God] was not any thing made that
was made.

We must always remember that only God was in
the beginning as stated in Genesis 1:1. God was the
sole mover.

John 1:4:
In him [God] was life; and the life was the light
of men.

What was this life which was in God and which was
the light of men? This life was the Spirit of God
which is the light of God given in concretion. This
spirit of God was upon all the prophets who spoke
and wrote God's mind and will. Finally it was upon
Jesus Christ Himself.* The spirit of God was spiritual
revelation from God to men of God. Not everything
that God revealed to the prophets was written down.
Prophets frequently spoke the Word of God and then
did not write it down. Other times the prophets
wrote down what they spoke. Some of the spoken
Word of the prophets we do not have, but the Word
we do have in writing was and still is "the light of
men."

*Mark 1:10: "And straightway coming up out of the water, he saw the
heavens opened, and the Spirit like a dove descending upon him."

32

II Peter 1:21:
For the prophecy came not in old time by the will of man: but holy men of God spake *as they were* moved by the Holy Ghost.

Not everything that God has revealed to man is recorded in the Bible, but that which is needed for salvation and for our learning is recorded. This is the meaning of the record in John 1:4, "... and the life was the light of men." The revelation came to men of God who spoke as they were moved by the Holy Spirit; they either uttered it verbally and/or made it known by way of writing, thus "holy men of God spake."*

John 1:5:
And the light [God, I John 1:5] shineth in darkness; and the darkness comprehended it not.

How did the light shine in darkness before the coming of Jesus Christ? By way of the men of God who spoke or wrote God's mind and will. The written Word continues today to shine in the darkness of this world. Darkness cannot bring forth light, neither can darkness overcome light. One small candle is powerful enough to penetrate and dispel darkness. So also is

*II Timothy 3:16: "All scripture *is* given by inspiration of God [*theopneustos*, God-breathed] ....
Galatians 1:11,12: "But I certify you, brethren, that the gospel which was preached of me is not after man. For I neither received it of man, neither was I taught *it*, but by the revelation of Jesus Christ."

God's revelation of Himself in His Word — "the darkness comprehended it not," the darkness could not quench the light.

> John 1:6–8:
> There was a man sent [commissioned] from God, whose name *was* John.
>
> The same [John] came for a witness, to bear witness of the Light [God], that all *men* through him [John] might believe.
>
> He [John] was not that Light [God], but *was sent* to bear witness of that Light [God].

The ministry of John is given in these three verses. God commissioned John for a special purpose of bearing witness. He came specifically to carry forth the sender's message.

> John 1:9:
> *That* was the true Light [God], which lighteth every man that cometh into the world.

God is the "true light." How does God "light" every man who comes into the world? By His revealed Word. God's revealed Word continues to light every man, even the unbeliever. Without the "true light," there would be total, impenetrable darkness in this world.

The focal point of these opening verses in the Gospel of John sets before us with utmost clarity the centrality of God. We note the added emphasis on God in the verses following.

John 1:10–12:
He [God] was in the world [by the revealed Word], and the world was made by him [God], and the world knew him [God] not.

He [God] came unto his own [to Israel by the revealed Word spoken and written, and later in Jesus Christ], and his own [Israel] received him [the revealed Word both spoken and written, and later Jesus Christ] not.

But as many as received him [God, by the revealed Word spoken and written, and later in Jesus Christ], to them gave he [God] power [*exousia,* to exercise the privilege] to become the sons of God, *even* to them that believe on [unto] his name [namesake, Jesus Christ].

A literal translation of verse 12 would be, "But as many as walked according to the revealed Word given to the prophets and later the revealed Word, Jesus Christ, to them God gave the privilege of adoption as sons of God, to those who continued believing unto the name of Jesus Christ." The word "on" is the preposition *eis,* meaning "unto." Euclid, the mathematician, used the word *eis,* meaning motion along a line from a starting point to the point at which one wished to arrive. This is its usage in this verse: "... to them who continue believing unto [continuously continue to believe on] his name ...." Israel remained as adopted sons only so long as they continued believing. The Israelites were not sons of God by birth but when Israel believed "unto [*eis*] His name," God adopted them as sons.

"*Even* to them that believe on his name" refers to the name of Jesus Christ which is above every other human name. He, Jesus Christ, was the "namesake" of God, which name relates back to the source of all life, God.

> John 1:13:
> Which were [who was] born [conceived], not of blood, nor of the will of the flesh, nor of the will of man, but of God.

The first word, "which," must be the word "who," referring to the "namesake" of verse 12, Jesus Christ. The word "born" is the same word as "begotten": "Who was born [begotten], not of blood ...." You and I are born of blood. All Israel was born of blood. Hebrews 2:14 says, "... children are partakers of flesh and blood ...." The only one who did not partake as the natural man in the life of the flesh, which is in the blood, was Jesus Christ. Therefore, John 1:13 refers only to Jesus Christ. It was Jesus Christ "who was born, not of blood, nor of the will of the flesh, nor of the will of man, but of God." Jesus Christ's existence began when He was conceived by God's creating the soul-life of Jesus in Mary. God created, brought into existence, this life in an ovum in Mary's womb.

There are a number of different Greek words used in the Bible for "will." *Thelēma* is the Greek word used in this verse: "nor of the will [*thelēma*] of the flesh." *Thelēma* means "to desire or anticipate but not to determine." In this verse *thelēma* is a wonderful usage, far beyond what we realize when we first read it. "Which were [Who was] born not of blood, nor of the will [*thelēma*] of the flesh, nor of the will [*thelēma*] of man ...." Man might desire or anticipate the Christ, but man could not will, determine, Jesus Christ's birth. Man could never say, "Now I am going to produce the Christ," because Jesus Christ was not born according to the will [*thelēma*] of the flesh ...." Every woman had the physical potential to bring forth Jesus Christ, but the will of a human being could not determine this bringing forth of Jesus the Christ because He was born by the will, the determination of God.

John 1:14:

And the Word [revealed Word — Jesus Christ] was made flesh [the conception], and dwelt among us [His birth nine months later], (and we beheld his glory, the glory as of the only begotten of the Father,) full of grace and truth.

We beheld [intently observed] his [Jesus Christ's] glory [greatness]. Jesus Christ always did the will of the Father.* Jesus Christ in the flesh declared God unto mankind.† Jesus Christ, the promised One, was the only-begotten of the Father because God created soul-life in the womb of a woman only once.

John 1:18:

No man hath seen God at any time; the only begotten Son, which is in the bosom of the Father, he hath declared [*exēgeomai*, made known] *him.*

---

*John 4:34: "Jesus saith unto them, My meat is to do the will of him that sent me, and to finish his work."

John 6:38: "For I came down from heaven, not to do mine own will, but the will of him that sent me."

John 8:29: "And he that sent me is with me: the Father hath not left me alone; for I do always those things that please him."

Luke 2:49: "And he said unto them, How is it that ye sought me? wist ye not that I must be about my Father's business?"

†I John 1:2: "For the life was manifested, and we have seen *it*, and bear witness, and shew unto you that eternal life, which was with the Father, and was manifested unto us."

"In the bosom" is an Oriental idiom meaning love, comfort and rest.* Jesus Christ was in the bosom of the Father, in the foreknowledge of God. Jesus Christ, the only-begotten Son was in the bosom, in the love, comfort and in the rest of the Father who knew all from the beginning. Jesus Christ then made known the Father.

In a study on "Who Is the Word," in addition to the opening verses in the Gospel of John, we must also consider the following Scriptures.

As noted previously, Jesus Christ's existence began when God created soul-life in the womb of Mary.

> John 3:13:
> And no man hath ascended up to heaven, but he that came down from heaven, *even* the Son of man which is in heaven.

"Came down from heaven" was the conception or creation of life in the womb of Mary for the Son of man.

Colossians 1:14–18 contains a figure of speech which must be carefully noted for a clear understanding of God's Word.

*Note II Samuel 12:3; Isaiah 40:11; Luke 16:22; John 13:23.

Colossians 1:14,15:
In whom [Jesus Christ] we have redemption
through his blood, *even* the forgiveness [*aphesin,*
remission] of sins:

Who [Jesus Christ] is the image of the invisible
God, the firstborn of every creature.

God is invisible because He is Spirit. Jesus Christ
was visible; He was the image spiritually of the
invisible God; and, being in concretion, He did
declare the Father who is God.

Verses 16 and 17 of Colossians 1 are a parenthetical phrase, a figure of speech which is an
explanation. When a parenthesis is employed, one
must proceed in reading from the last word preceding
the parenthesis to the first word after the parenthesis.
No thought continuity is lost, and the truth is quickly
evident.

Reading from the last word of verse 15 directly on
to verse 18 without reading the parenthesis of verses
16 and 17 will give the following statement.

Verse 15:
Who [Jesus Christ] is the image of the invisible
God, the firstborn of every creature:

Verse 18:
And he [Jesus Christ] is the head of the body,
the church ....

The parenthetical verses, 16 and 17, refer to what
God did.

Colossians 1:16,17:
For by him [God] were all things created, that
are in heaven, and that are in earth, visible and
invisible, whether *they be* thrones, or dominions,
or principalities, or powers: all things were
created by him [God], and for him [God]:

And he [God] is before all things, and by him
[God] all things consist [cohere, were created].

The people who say that all things were created by
Jesus Christ contradict the first verse of the Bible:
"In the beginning God created...."

Another example of a stumbling block is found in
John 10:30 where Jesus says, "I and *my* Father are
one." It has already been established that Jesus and
God are not one and the same. Jesus and God were
not one from the beginning, but they were one in
purpose as shown in the context of this verse as Jesus
declared His Father on earth. God and Jesus Christ's

unanimity of purpose is poignantly shown in that
Jesus Christ always did the Father's will* and finished
the work for which God had sent Him.†

Hebrews 1 contains another erroneously interpreted passage which must be "rightly divided" in our
study.

> Hebrews 1:1,2:
> God, who at sundry times [various times] and in
> divers [varied] manners [ways] spake in time
> past unto the fathers by the prophets.
>
> Hath in these last days [in this last time] spoken
> unto us by *his* Son, whom he [God] hath
> appointed heir of all things, by [for] whom also
> he made the worlds.

*John 4:34: "Jesus saith unto them, My meat is to do the will of him
that sent me, and to finish his work."

John 5:30: "I can of mine own self do nothing: as I hear, I judge: and
my judgment is just; because I seek not mine own will, but the will of
the Father which hath sent me."

John 6:38: "For I came down from heaven, not to do mine own will,
but the will of him that sent me."

†Hebrews 12:2: "Looking unto Jesus the author and finisher of *our*
faith; who for the joy that was set before him endured the cross,
despising the shame, and is set down at the right hand of the throne of
God."

John 5:36: "But I have greater witness than *that* of John: for the works
which the Father hath given me to finish, the same works that I do,
bear witness of me, that the Father hath sent me."

John 17:4: "I have glorified thee on the earth: I have finished the work
which thou gavest me to do."

John 19:30: "When Jesus therefore had received the vinegar, he said, It
is finished: and he bowed his head, and gave up the ghost."

Originally God created all things to His own satisfaction, knowing in His foreknowledge that His only-begotten Son would enjoy those things which God had created for Himself and for His appointed heir. "Worlds" is the Greek word *aion* meaning "ages." It is *for* Him, the Son, that the ages are made, not *by* Him.

> Ephesians 3:9:
> And to make all *men* see what *is* the fellowship [*oikonomia,* administration, in all texts except Stephens] of the mystery, which from the beginning of the world hath been hid in God, who created all things by [on account of, or for] Jesus Christ.

The words "by Jesus Christ" are only in one critical Greek text — Stephens. With these words in the text the preposition "by" would have to be rendered "for." The usage then would be precise.

Christians who believe the Bible and who rightly divide The Word have the true Word, and as such they will know that God is the Word, whom Jesus Christ declared. When we study The Word closely, we see how emphatically The Word corroborates itself. Instead of stumbling over Scriptures, we see by careful scrutiny the precision with which God has revealed Himself to us in His Word. All Scripture, especially Genesis 1:1; John 1:1—18; 10:30; Colossians 1:14—18; Hebrews 1:1,2; Ephesians 3:9, reveals the light of Truth which dispels darkness.

> "In the beginning was the Word [God], and the [revealed] Word [spoken and written, and later in Jesus Christ] was with God [in His fore-knowledge], and the Word was God."

CHAPTER THREE

Body, Soul, Spirit

Before we move into the depth of this important study we must understand some fundamental terms. When I speak of the man of body and soul, I speak of the man who is *not* born again of God's Spirit. This is the accurate Biblical usage of "natural man." The five senses are the only avenues of learning the natural man has. Everything that ever comes to a natural man's mind must come over one or a combination of these five senses: hearing, seeing, smelling, tasting, touching.

Our senses gather information from a source or sources outside ourselves. We come to conclusions from our accumulated exposure and experience, and thus we come to believe what we believe. Being aware of the process of learning, I came to the conclusion many years ago that for me the Word of God (not the King James Version, but *the* Word of God which was given when "... holy men of God spake *as they were* moved by the Holy Ghost") would be my source for truth.

45

For years I read around the Word of God, with the writers of outside works being centers of reference for me. Soon I suffered from a common disease called basic mental confusion because equally great men would contradict each other regarding the same verse of Scripture. When I began to consider the process of learning, I finally came to the conclusion that instead of spending my life in confusion because of the abundance of men's opinions I would accept *one* center of reference for truth which was outside myself. My center of reference for truth is the Word of God.

If the Word of God is wrong, I am going to be wrong; but if the Word of God is right, then I have everything to gain by taking it as my sole center of reference. I believe that The Word takes the place of the absent Christ and that the holy spirit is Christ in us by way of God's Word.* I believe that the Bible gives the truth regarding man's redemption and his dominion and authority and power over all God's creation. I believe that the Bible gives the truth regarding Jesus Christ, His coming, His death, His resurrection, His ascension; the Bible is God's stating of the truth regarding the new heaven and the new earth which God is going to establish. I believe that the Bible gives truth, not just facts. Anything man

*Romans 10:17: "So then faith *cometh* by hearing, and hearing by the word of God."

does, anything man makes, is a fact. I believe that the Word of God is Truth — Truth which is eternal, the same yesterday, today and forever. I believe that the revelation of the Word of God is an absolute necessity for the man of five senses, the natural man. If the senses man is going to be a complete man, he must have an accurate knowledge of God's Word.

A very condensed Scripture which we must thoroughly master to understand the origin of man is in Isaiah.

Isaiah 43:7:
Even [for] every one that is called by my name: for I have created him for my glory, I have formed him; yea, I have made him.

I have *created* him; I have *formed* him; I have *made* him. Are the three words "created," "formed" and "made" synonymous? Most people in my classes say yes, but if The Word means what it says and says what it means, these words cannot be synonymous. When God said formed, He meant *formed.* When He said made, He meant *made.* When He said created, He meant *created.* Had He meant formed all the way through, it would have said formed at all three places. But God says, "I created, formed and made man."

47

> I Thessalonians 5:23:
> And the very God of peace sanctify you wholly; and *I pray God* your whole spirit and soul and body be preserved blameless unto the coming of our Lord Jesus Christ.

Are these three words "spirit," "soul" and "body" synonymous? They are no more synonymous than are "created," "formed" and "made." Body means body, soul means soul and spirit means spirit. Now we must go to The Word and let The Word speak as to what is formed, what is made and what is created; and what is body, soul and spirit.

In the beginning man was formed, made and created. Let us follow the development of Scripture.

> Genesis 2:7:
> And the Lord God formed man *of* the dust of the ground ....

The Hebrew word for "formed" is *yatsar*, "to fashion out of something that is already in existence." Genesis 2:7 says that God formed man of the dust of the ground, a substance which already existed when God began working on man. The word "man" is *adam*, meaning "red earth." Man's body is composed of the same elements that are in the dust of the earth.

Genesis 3:19:
In the sweat of thy face shalt thou eat bread, till thou return unto the ground; for out of it wast thou taken: for dust thou *art*, and unto dust shalt thou return.

The body of man was formed (*yatsar*) of the dust of the ground. And, because of the natural law that everything must ultimately return to its original state, the body must return to dust. Ecclesiastes 3:20 says, "... all are of the dust, and all turn to dust again." This obviously refers to men's as well as animals' bodies.

The next word to observe is the word "soul" which in Hebrew is *nephesh*. What is soul? The soul in man is that which gives the body its life, its vitality.

Genesis 2:7:
And the Lord God formed man [man's body] *of* the dust of the ground, and breathed into his nostrils the breath of life; and man became a living soul.

"Breathed into his nostrils" is the figure of speech *condescensio.* God put life into Adam; He made man a living soul. The word "made" is in Hebrew *asah,* "a substance required of which the thing made consists." The soul is nothing more and nothing less than that

49

which gives life to a person's body. Sometimes it is called "the spirit of man." Soul has nothing to do with whether you are a Christian or a non-Christian. So long as a person breathes, he has a soul.

> I Peter 3:20:
> Which sometime were disobedient, when once the longsuffering of God waited in the days of Noah, while the ark was a preparing, wherein few, that is, eight souls were saved by water.

This verse is talking about the eight souls who were saved during the great flood. Were they Christians? No, Christ had not yet come. Noah, his wife and their three sons and their wives — all eight people, eight souls — were saved.

> Acts 27:37:
> And we were in all in the ship two hundred threescore and sixteen souls.

This record in Acts refers to the ship on which Paul and Luke were sailing to Rome. Except for Paul and Luke, the rest on board were unbelievers, non-Christians; and yet the record says, "and we were in all in the ship two hundred threescore and sixteen souls." "Soul" means alive people; soul is that part which gives life to the body.

50

The confusion between the soul and the spirit has caused no end of difficulty for people. They say the soul is immortal, for instance. They talk about transmigration of the soul, the immortality of the soul. These are all erroneous usages of words concerning subjects which are set with exactness and precision in the Word of God.

Genesis 1:30:
And to every beast of the earth, and to every fowl of the air, and to every thing that creepeth upon the earth, wherein *there is* life ....

The word "life" is "soul." This verse says that every beast has a living soul.

Genesis 1:20:
And God said, Let the waters bring forth abundantly the moving creature that hath life ....

Where there is a soul in an animal, there is movement, there is breath-life.

Genesis 1:21:
And God created great whales, and every living creature [soul] ....

Genesis 1:24:
And God said, Let the earth bring forth the living creature ....

51

The word "creature" is again the word "soul." These are some of the places in Genesis 1 where the word "soul" is used regarding creatures as well as man. The soul, then, is that which gives a being its life. The word *nephesh* is "soul." *Chai* means "moving" life, "moving" soul. *Nephesh chai* is always used in the Word of God as living life or living soul, in contrast to a dead soul, a soul that has perished.

The modern church has been illogical on this particular issue because it usually teaches that the soul is spirit and goes back to God; but then these teachers deny that the soul of a cow (for a cow has soul-life) must also go back to God when that cow dies. If the soul came from God, it must ultimately go back to God, just as the body of man must ultimately go back to dust from which it came. God is Spirit. Is the soul spirit? No. The soul is that which gives one breath-life.*

God *made* every beast wherein there is a soul, a life. The question we must now ask is where is the soul-life of man. Leviticus tells us.

Leviticus 17:11:
For the life of the flesh *is* in the blood ....

---

*Previously "soul" was defined as "breath-life." Plants do not have breath-life and yet they obviously have life in that they grow and bear fruit. Plants have growth-life, but they do not have breath-life. Animals have both growth-life and soul-life or breath-life.

The soul-life is in the blood and is passed on to the next generation when the sperm impregnates the egg at the time of fertilization.

What ultimately happens to the soul? Soul-life is passed on from one person to his progeny. If a person has no offspring, his soul is simply gone when he dies; it is no more. There is nothing immortal about the soul, no more so than there is anything immortal about dust. Man's body is made of dust and it goes back to dust. Man's soul-life which comes from his predecessors simply is no more after he has taken his last breath.

After studying "formed" and "made," we still must consider the Biblical usage of the word "created." What part of man was created?

To find the first use of "create" we look at the first verse in the Bible.

Genesis 1:1:
In the beginning God created the heaven and the earth.

"To create" literally means "to bring something out of nothing" or "to bring into existence something which never existed before."

53

Many Sunday school teachers say that "on the first day God *created* thus and so, and on the second day God *created* something else," and so on. That is not what the Word of God says. In verse 3 God said, "Let there be light." Why didn't He have to create it? Because whatever light is composed of had already been created when God in the beginning created the heaven and the earth. All He had to do was "speak" these other things into existence. Verse 6 says, "And God said ...." Verse 9, "And God said ...." Verse 11, "And God said ...." Verse 14, "And God said ...."

In verse 21 God *created* "great whales, and every living creature that moveth ...." Their bodies were brought forth or formed out of the waters. Water and earth already existed, so the substance which made up their bodies didn't have to be created. Then what had to be created at this point? Soul-life, because it never existed before. As recorded in verses 24–26, God brought forth from the earth the cattle, the beasts and man — all being given the soul-life that was created in verse 21. As you remember, God simply *made* life for man, He used the life which had been previously created.

As God progressed in this work of forming, making and creating the earth and its inhabitants, He finally came to bringing about His culminating work — man.

54

Genesis 1:27:
So God created man in his *own* image, in the
image of God created he him; male and female
created he them.

God had already formed and made man; man
already had a body and soul. So what was God doing
when He created man in His own image? What is the
image of God?

John 4:24:
God *is* a Spirit ....

God created within man spirit, His image. Thus
man became body, soul and spirit. After God created
within man His own image, God had a com-
panion — not in the body and soul parts of man, but
in the spirit. It is that part of man which made it
possible for God to talk to man and for man to
communicate with God. This gave them fellowship.
We read about the threefold man in Isaiah and
Thessalonians where the Scriptures say that man was
formed, made and created, and that he was body
soul and spirit. Scientists today talk about creating
life. That is a misnomer. They may rediscover,
revamp, reorganize, readapt or recompound; but they
cannot create because to create is to bring something
into existence which did not previously exist.
Scientists always start with some substance so they
are not *creating*.

Man, as he originally was put together, surpassed the animal realm in that he not only had body and soul, but also spirit. It was the spirit which set man apart from the rest of creation. Because of man's having spirit, God could communicate with his final masterpiece.

Again we can see that God in His Word meant what He said and said what He meant. In the beginning God formed the body of man, He made the soul of man and He created the spirit in man.

CHAPTER FOUR

The Unforgivable Sin

Regarding the subject of the unforgivable sin, also called the sin against the Holy Ghost or blasphemy against the Holy Ghost,* we must begin by understanding that there are two spiritual seeds. Genesis has the foundational Scripture.

> Genesis 3:15:
> And I [God] will put enmity between thee [serpent, devil] and the woman, and between thy seed and her seed; it [the woman's seed] shall bruise thy head, and thou [devil's seed] shalt bruise his heel.

The victor in this confrontation will obviously be the seed of the woman. What is the significance of seed? Seed is necessary in order to beget children, in order to bear fruit. A child cannot be born physically

---

*Holy Ghost is *pneuma hagion*, Holy Spirit. King James Version has Holy Ghost 89 times and Holy Spirit 4 times. In our day the word "Spirit" communicates more exactly the true meaning rather than "Ghost."

without seed first being planted in the mother's womb. Once this seed is planted, the resulting fruit cannot be altered. You are the result of the seed of your earthly father as long as you live. But Genesis 3:15 speaks of a woman having seed. What is "her seed"? Galatians 3:16 clarifies "her seed" in saying, "... And to thy seed, which is Christ."

So it is spiritually. In order to be born spiritually (called "being born again"), seed must be planted. A spiritual seed cannot be changed any more than a physical seed can be changed.

The Word of God tells us that there are two spiritual fathers and, therefore, two possible sources for seed: God, the Father of our Lord and Savior Jesus Christ, and the devil, the god of this world. Thus a person can spiritually be born of either one of these two fathers. To observe the result of either of these two spiritual seeds being planted in man, let us take a hypothetical case — John Doe.

John Doe is born a man of body and soul — a natural man who has physical seed. However, he has no spiritual seed in him. When John Doe, a man of body and soul, confesses with his mouth Jesus as Lord and believes that God raised Him from the dead (according to the command of Romans 10:9 and 10),

he is born again with God's seed (Christ)* in him.
God's seed (Christ) is spirit, thus John Doe is now a
man of body, soul and spirit — spirit which is eternal
and which is life.

However, there is another possibility. Rather than
confessing Jesus as his Lord, John Doe could believe
that the devil is the true God. John Doe, confessing
the devil with his mouth and accepting the devil as his
lord, is born again. This spiritual seed which is born
within is the seed of the devil. Once John Doe is born
of the devil's seed, he can never rid himself of it for
this seed, like all seed, is permanent. This acceptance
of the devil as lord is the unforgivable sin — it can
never be rooted out.

The Epistle of I John distinguishes between for-
givable sins and the unforgivable sin.

> I John 5:16:
> If any man see his brother sin a sin *which is* not
> unto death, he shall ask, and he shall give him
> life for them that sin not unto death. There is a
> sin unto death: I do not say that he shall pray
> for it.

Praying for John Doe after he has confessed the
devil as his lord is useless. God can no more take the

---

*Galatians 3:16b: "... He saith not, And to seeds, as of many; but as of
one, And to thy seed, which is Christ."

devil's seed out of John Doe than He can take His own seed out of a man once that man has confessed and believed in Jesus Christ as Lord. It is futile to pray for forgiveness from the "sin unto death" for that sin is seed and cannot be changed.

It *is* possible for a man of body and soul to go through life and never be born again of either seed. A person does not always make a choice. But if he does, he has only two alternatives. A man can either accept Jesus Christ as his Lord, or he can accept the devil as his lord. There is a complete separation between the households of the two gods. They are opposite forces and antithetical essences. Once one of these gods is accepted, nothing can be done to eradicate the seed or to change the consequences. The seed and its inherent qualities are permanent.

All four Gospels have records of the unforgivable sin. Jesus spoke to the Pharisees and explained the unforgivable sin to these outwardly religious leaders.

> Matthew 12:31:
> Wherefore I say unto you, All manner of sin and blasphemy shall be forgiven unto men: but the blasphemy *against* the *Holy* Ghost shall not be forgiven unto men.

> Mark 3:29:
> But he that shall blaspheme against the Holy

Ghost hath never forgiveness ....

Why? Because that person is born of the seed of the serpent. Luke also speaks of blaspheming against the Holy Ghost.

Luke 12:10:
And whosoever shall speak a word against the Son of man [against Christ], it shall be forgiven him: but unto him that blasphemeth against the Holy Ghost it shall not be forgiven.

A full and interesting account of Jesus' teaching of the unforgivable sin is recorded in John 8.

John 8:2:
And early in the morning he [Jesus] came again into the temple, and all the people came unto him; and he sat down, and taught them [the scribes and Pharisees].

These were the same scribes and Pharisees spoken of in Matthew, Mark and Luke. They were the ones who had committed the "sin against the Holy Ghost," "blasphemy against the Holy Ghost," the "unforgivable sin." Note the argument as it developed.

John 8:12–19:
Then spake Jesus again unto them [the Phari-

61

sees], saying, I am the light of the world: he that followeth me shall not walk in darkness, but shall have the light of life.

The Pharisees therefore said unto him, Thou bearest record of thyself; thy record is not true.

Jesus answered and said unto them, Though I bear record of myself, *yet* my record is true: for I know whence I came, and whither I go; but ye cannot tell whence I come, and whither I go.

Ye judge after the flesh; I judge no man.

And yet if I judge, my judgment is true: for I am not alone, but I and the Father that sent me.

It is also written in your law, that the testimony of two men is true.

I am one that bear witness of myself, and the Father that sent me beareth witness of me.

Then said they unto him, Where is thy Father? Jesus answered, Ye neither know me, nor my Father: if ye had known me, ye should have known my Father also.

Jesus said in addressing the rulers of the temple,

the religious leaders, "You Pharisees do not even know my Father." What leadership!

John 8:20,21:
These words spake Jesus in the treasury, as he taught in the temple: and no man laid hands on him; for his hour was not yet come.

Then said Jesus again unto them, I go my way, and ye shall seek me, and shall die in your sins: whither I go, ye cannot come.

There must have been a profound reason for Jesus to use such strong language.

Verse 22:
Then said the Jews,* Will he kill himself? because he saith, Whither I go, ye cannot come.

When people are born again of the wrong seed, they cannot be taught spiritual truths for they cannot understand; the eyes of their understanding are closed. The Pharisees said, "Will he kill himself?" They thought that if a person killed himself he would go to hell. This was clever reasoning since the Pharisees were certain that they themselves were heaven-bound. How wrong people can be and still think they are right!

*The word "Jew" and its derivatives, as used in the King James Version, should always be understood as meaning "Judean" or "of the Judean religion." The word "Jew" was never used in any text until 1775.

John 8:23–29:

And he [Jesus] said unto them, Ye are from [of the] beneath; I am from above: ye are of this world; I am not of this world.

I said therefore unto you, that ye shall die in your sins: for if ye believe not that I am *he*, ye shall die in your sins.

Then said they unto him, Who art thou? And Jesus saith unto them, Even *the same* that I said unto you from the beginning.

I have many things to say and to judge of you: but he that sent me is true; and I speak to the world those things which I have heard of him.

They understood not that he spake to them of the Father.

Then said Jesus unto them, When ye have lifted up the Son of man, then shall ye know that I am *he*, and *that* I do nothing of myself; but as my Father hath taught me, I speak these things.

And he that sent me is with me: the Father hath not left me alone; for I do always those things that please him.

Why did Jesus bother to tell these great truths when He obviously knew that He could never convert the Pharisees who were already born of the seed of the devil? He gave this information because of the other people present in the Temple; they were fertile ground.

John 8:30—38:
As he spake these words, many believed on him.

Then said Jesus to those Jews which believed on him, If ye continue in my word, *then* are ye my disciples indeed;

And ye shall know the truth, and the truth shall make you free.

They [the Pharisees] answered him, We be Abraham's seed, and were never in bondage to any man [Yet at that very time they were in bondage under the Romans!]: how sayest thou, Ye shall be made free?

Jesus answered them ....

I know that ye are Abraham's seed [according to the flesh, their physical bloodline]; but ye seek to kill me, because my word hath no place in you.

65

I speak that which I have seen with my Father: and ye do that which ye have seen with your father.

There are two different fathers mentioned: one is the God and Father of the Lord Jesus Christ and the other father is the devil. Those people whom the devil fathers are his children. Those whom the true God fathers are His children. Note the impact of the next verse.

John 8:39:
They [the Pharisees] answered and said unto him, Abraham is our father. Jesus saith unto them, If ye were Abraham's children, ye would do the works of Abraham.

How could Jesus in verse 37 agree with the Pharisees that they were of Abraham's seed, and in verse 39 turn and differ with them saying, "If ye were Abraham's children ..."? Verse 37 refers to the Pharisees as being of Abraham's bloodline, whereas verse 39 is speaking of Abrahamic believers. The Pharisees could claim Abraham as their ancestor; but they did not believe in God as Abraham did and, therefore, they were not in the line of believers as Abraham was — in contrast to what the Pharisees believed of themselves. The heated discussion continued.

John 8:40,41:

But now ye seek to kill me, a man that hath told you the truth, which I have heard of God: this did not Abraham.

Ye do the deeds of your father. Then said they to him, We be not born of fornication; we have one Father, *even* God.

The Pharisees surely sounded religious. They truly sounded sincere; but sincerity is no guarantee for truth. The Pharisees said, "We have one Father, *even* God." When people say, "We have a Father," it is important to find out *which* father, *which* God, for there are two. To accept the Lord Jesus Christ as Savior is one birth; to have the devil as one's father is totally different.

As Jesus and the Pharisees conversed, the Pharisees became increasingly irritated and so resorted to personal attacks on Jesus. They slammed Jesus by saying, "We be not born of fornication." These Pharisees believed Jesus was an illegitimate child. The Pharisees boasted that they were not conceived out of wedlock; and then they continued by boasting that they had one father, even God. They neglected to say which god, so Jesus clarified this for them.

Verse 42—44:

Jesus said unto them, If God were your Father,

67

ye would love me: for I proceeded forth and came from God; neither came I of myself, but he sent me.

Why do ye not understand my speech? *even* because ye cannot hear my word.

Ye are of *your* father the devil [Could anyone write it more plainly? Could it be more clear?], and the lusts of your father ye will do. He was a murderer from the beginning, and abode not in the truth, because there is no truth in him. When he speaketh a lie, he speaketh of his own: for he is a liar, and the father of it.

"Ye are of *your* father the devil ...." These religious leaders had accepted the devil as their father, the unforgivable sin of which they could never repent. Once the devil's seed is born within, it can never be withdrawn. The Pharisees of John 8 were permanently and irrevocably the children of the devil.

A point of confusion arises concerning seed when occasionally followers of Christ claim that since they are born again of God's seed, they can no longer sin. These people usually quote I John 3:9 as their substantiating Scripture. Let us read this passage in its proper context.

I John 3:9,10 and 12:
Whosoever is born of God doth not commit sin;
for his [God's] seed remaineth in him: and he
cannot sin [Where? In that of which he is born,
spirit], because he is born of God.

In this the children of God are manifest, and the
children of the devil ...

Not as Cain, *who* was of that wicked one [the
devil] ....

I John 3 says that a man cannot sin in the seed
which he has accepted. The context does not even
suggest that a person, once born of God's seed,
cannot sin in the flesh. God's seed remains sinless; but
a saved man must work on perfecting the actions of
the flesh.

The context of I John 3 also explains why God did
not receive Cain's offering as recorded in Genesis 4.
Cain was "of that wicked one." He was born of the
seed of the devil and thus could have nothing to do
with God. Because he was "of that wicked one," Cain
could actually hate his brother. Hate is a manifestation of the seed of the devil. When a man is born of
the seed of the devil, he has the hate of the devil.
When a man is born of the seed of Christ, he has love
in the spirit that is within. *True* hate and *true* love

begin as qualities inherent in spiritual seed; they are characteristic of their respective fathers.

How clearly the Word of God explains life to us. The unforgivable sin, the seed of the devil being born within a man, is Biblically accurate and, therefore, makes sense. Seed cannot be changed; so, when a person accepts the seed of the devil, he has it eternally, even as one who accepts the seed of God the Father of our Lord Jesus Christ has His seed eternally. One seed means eternal life; the other, eternal damnation. Man's freedom of will permits him to choose the seed he wants and thus determine his own destiny.

CHAPTER FIVE

Sons of God: Adoption and Birth

There are two ways to acquire a son: by adoption and by birth. A son by adoption is one who has been legally taken into a family. A son by birth is one who has the seed of the father of the family in him.

In the Old Testament the "sons of God" refer to those whom God legally transacted to adopt. Those people who believed were made God's adopted sons.

> Romans 9:4:
> Who are Israelites; to whom *pertaineth* the adoption, and the glory, and the covenants, and the giving of the law, and the service *of God,* and the promises.

> Exodus 4:22:
> And thou shalt say unto Pharaoh, Thus saith the Lord, Israel *is* my son, *even* my firstborn.

In the Old Testament Israel represented the believers' line, the sons of God. The Israelites who believed God were set aside as a distinctive people.

71

Deuteronomy 14:1,2:
Ye *are* the children of the Lord your God ....

For thou *art* an holy people unto the Lord thy God, and the Lord hath chosen thee to be a peculiar people unto himself, above all the nations that *are* upon the earth.

The believers of Israel were adopted, and thus made heirs to God's inheritance. His children, Israel, He would also protect and nurture.

Deuteronomy 32:8,9:
When the most High divided to the nations their inheritance, when he separated the sons of Adam, he set the bounds of the people according to the number of the children of Israel.

For the Lord's portion *is* his people; Jacob* is the lot of his inheritance.

Jeremiah 31:9:
They shall come with weeping, and with supplications will I lead them: I will cause them to walk by the rivers of waters in a straight way, wherein they shall not stumble: for I am a father to Israel, and Ephraim* *is* my firstborn.

*The head man or current leader is used as the figure of speech *synechoche* → part put for the whole. Jacob, the head man represents all Israel. In Jeremiah 31:9 Ephraim represents Israel.

Sons of God: Adoption and Birth

First God adopted Israel; then He gave them all the benefits of a son: He considered them a special people, He was concerned for their welfare, and He made them heirs to His inheritance. After being given these provisions, God's adopted sons could still live a life of their own choosing. According to the many accounts in The Word, Israel still stumbled along — sometimes obedient to their Father's will and sometimes not. One such example is recorded in Numbers 33. The children of Israel were admonished to marry within their own selected people. But sons didn't and still don't always behave, thus bringing problems to themselves.

Numbers 33:50-54:
And the Lord spake unto Moses in the plains of Moab by Jordan *near* Jericho, saying,

Speak unto the children of Israel, and say unto them, When ye are passed over Jordan into the land of Canaan;

Then ye shall drive out all the inhabitants of the land from before you, and destroy all their pictures, and destroy all their molten images, and quite pluck down all their high places [temples to worship other gods]:

> And ye shall dispossess *the inhabitants of* the land, and dwell therein: for I have given you the land to possess it.
>
> And ye shall divide the land by lot for an inheritance among your families: *and* to the more ye shall give the more inheritance, and to the fewer ye shall give the less inheritance: every man's *inheritance* shall be in the place where his lot falleth; according to the tribes of your fathers ye shall inherit.

Why did God tell Israel to cast down the idols in the land? Because these idols existed for the unbelievers; and God's people were a unique, peculiar people and were not to carry on as the unbelievers, the unrighteous, did.

> Verse 55:
> But if ye will not drive out the inhabitants of the land from before you; then it shall come to pass, that those which ye let remain of them *shall be* pricks in your eyes, and thorns in your sides, and shall vex you in the land wherein ye dwell.

If the believers allowed any of the unbelieving people to remain in the land, the believing sons would marry the daughters of the unbelievers: the "sons of

74

God" would marry the "daughters of men," just as happened before and is recorded in Genesis 6.

> Genesis 6:1,2:
> And it came to pass, when men began to multiply on the face of the earth, and daughters were born unto them,
>
> That the sons of God saw the daughters of men that they *were* fair; and they took them wives of all which they chose.

Theological teaching has propounded that the "sons of God" in Genesis 6 are angels and the "daughters of men" are the daughters of human beings living upon the earth. Thus the teaching conjectures that the race of giants, in Hebrew called *nephilim,* came from the cohabitation between angels and humans. This idea is strictly private interpretation; the Bible suggests no such thing. The Word of God explicitly tells who these two specified groups are: the sons of God and the daughters of men. The first group stems from Seth and can be traced like a red thread all through The Word. The latter group stems from Cain.

> I John 3:12:
> Not as Cain, *who* was of that wicked one, and slew his brother. And wherefore slew he him? Because his own works were evil, and his brother's righteous.

Because Cain was born of the devil's seed he was accursed of God and his offering could not be accepted. Genesis 4 tells of Cain's treatment.

> Genesis 4:14 and 16:
> Behold, thou hast driven me [Cain] out this day from the face of the earth; and from thy face shall I be hid [Cain was an unbeliever, one who was absolutely unrighteous. This is why he says]; and I shall be a fugitive and a vagabond in the earth ....
>
> And Cain went out from the presence of the Lord ....

The specific kind of unrighteousness which Cain committed was unacceptable and unforgivable. Thus the unrighteousness of Cain represented all the unbelievers in the Bible during Old Testament times. On the other hand, Cain's brother Seth was accepted of God.

> Genesis 4:26:
> And to Seth, to him also there was born a son; and he called his name Enos: then began men to call upon the name of the Lord.*

Seth and his son Enos were God-fearing men.

---

*"Enos" means "frail." The literal translation reads, "Then began men to call their idols or gods Jehovah." In Enos' day the profanation of the name of Jehovah took root.

Their line represented the believers, the called of God, the righteous ones.*

Although Seth and his offspring were faithful and righteous, Cain and his offspring, also adding to the population of the earth, had corrupted it by Noah's time.

> Genesis 6:1,2:
>
> And it came to pass, when men began to multiply [in wickedness] on the face of the earth, and daughters were born unto them,
>
> That the sons of God saw the daughters of men that they *were* fair; and they took them wives of all which they chose.

The sons of God, the believers, came out of the Seth line, the righteous ones. The daughters of men, the unbelievers, came out of the line of Cain, the unrighteous. God as their Father advised the children of Israel, Seth's progeny, to marry only the righteous. When Israel disobeyed and married Cain's progeny, they brought disaster to themselves.

God's sons, just like our earthly children, do not always live the best way. But when the children of

* Following the believers' family tree in Genesis 5; Seth begot Enos, Enos begot Cainan, Cainan begot Mahalaleel, Mahalaleel begot Jared, Jared begot Enoch, Enoch begot Methuselah, Methuselah begot Lamech, and Lamech begot Noah. And, according to Genesis 6:8, "Noah found grace in the eyes of the Lord."

Israel lived according to their Father's will, the adopted sons lived with power and victory.

> Hebrews 11:33-39:
> Who [Israel] through faith [believing] subdued kingdoms, wrought righteousness, obtained promises, stopped the mouths of lions,
>
> Quenched the violence of fire, escaped the edge of the sword, out of weakness were made strong, waxed valiant in fight, turned to flight the armies of the aliens.
>
> Women received their dead raised to life again: and others were tortured, not accepting deliverance; that they might obtain a better resurrection:
>
> And others had trial of *cruel* mockings and scourgings, yea, moreover of bonds and imprisonment:
>
> They were stoned, they were sawn asunder, were tempted, were slain with the sword: they wandered about in sheepskins and goatskins; being destitute, afflicted, tormented;
>
> (Of whom the world was not worthy:) they wandered in deserts, and *in* mountains, and *in* dens and caves of the earth.
>
> And these all, having obtained a good report

through faith [believing], received not the promise.

All these men, because they believed, accomplished and survived many things, but they received not the promise. They could not receive the promise, for Jesus Christ had not yet come to fulfill the law. The Old Testament believers looked forward to the Savior's coming, for as Jesus said of David, "He [David] saw my day." Even though David lived hundreds of years before Jesus' coming, David anticipated "the day" as he believed in the coming of the Holy One. So as David and the other believers trusted in what God promised, they were accounted righteous. They were adopted as sons. God adopted them.

II Corinthians 6:17:
Wherefore come out from among them, and be ye separate, saith the Lord, and touch not the unclean *thing*; and I will receive you.

In the Old Testament times God said that His adopted children, Israel, were a peculiar people unto Him.* So also in the New Testament, those who are

*Deuteronomy 14:2: "For thou *art* an holy people unto the Lord thy God, and the Lord hath chosen thee to be a peculiar people unto himself, above all the nations that *are* upon the earth."
Deuteronomy 26:18: "And the Lord hath avouched thee this day to be his peculiar people, as he hath promised thee, and that *thou* shouldest keep all his commandments."

The Law and Order of God

God's people are a separated, a peculiar people.* We who are born again are a peculiar people to Him because He has called us. In the Old Testament Israel was adopted as sons; but after Pentecost, we are sons because we have seed born within. The most critical question at this point is: Why did God adopt His Old Testament sons while He put His seed in His sons of the Church administration? God couldn't put seed in His children in the Old Testament because Christ had not made seed available. Therefore, adoption was the only way to acquire sons.

God's actions are limited by man's believing. And Mary the mother of Jesus was the first woman who believed to the extent that God could create soul-life in her so that she could bring forth God's only-begotten Son. After Christ had fulfilled the law, God's seed in Christ made possible sonship by birth† for believers. This type of birth is called being "born again," literally "born from above,"† and having "eternal life." "Born again" is found solely in the New Testament.

*Titus 2:4: "That they may teach the young women to be sober, to love their husbands, to love their children."
I Peter 2:9: "But ye *are* a chosen generation, a royal priesthood, an holy nation, a peculiar people; that ye should shew forth the praises of him who hath called you out of darkness into his marvellous light."

†This birth is called born again. The Greek word for "again" is *anothen* meaning "from above," spiritual birth, "born from above."

80

Galatians 4:7:
Wherefore thou art no more a servant, but a son; and if a son, then an heir of God through Christ.

I Peter tells a characteristic of God's seed in Christ which a person receives when he is born again.

I Peter 1:23:
Being born again, not of corruptible seed, but of incorruptible, by the word of God, which liveth and abideth forever.

When we were born physically, we had seed in us. When we were born again, we received another seed. The difference is that the seed with the second birth is incorruptible.

Eternal life, God's seed in Christ in us, becomes ours when we are born again of God's Spirit. What happens to bring this about? Ephesians 2 speaks on this subject.

Ephesians 2:5-9:
Even when we were dead in sins [dead because God's Spirit was not within], hath quickened us together with Christ, (by grace ye are saved;)

And hath raised *us* up together, and made *us* sit together in heavenly *places* in Christ Jesus:

81

That in the ages to come he might shew the exceeding riches of his grace in *his* kindness toward us through Christ Jesus.

For by grace are ye saved through faith [the faith of Jesus Christ]; and that not of yourselves: *it is* the gift of God:

Not of works, lest any man should boast.

Romans 10 tells how it is possible for a body-and-soul man who is dead in trespasses and sins and without God and without hope to be made alive.

Romans 10:17:
So then faith *cometh* by hearing, and hearing by the word of God.

What faith? The faith of Jesus Christ. And the faith of Jesus Christ comes when the man of body and soul hears the Word of God and believes. The step that must be taken is told in Romans.

Romans 10:9:
That if thou shalt confess with thy mouth the Lord Jesus, and shalt believe in thine heart that God hath raised him from the dead, thou shalt be saved.

Of all the great religious leaders there is only one

who was raised from the dead and that is Jesus Christ.
The proof that He is God's only-begotten son is that
God raised Jesus from the dead. Do you accept Jesus
as your Lord? Have you confessed it with your
mouth? The Word says that *you are saved.*

> Romans 10:10:
> For with the heart man believeth unto right-
> eousness; and with the mouth confession is
> made unto salvation.

The moment I fulfill these two requirements —
believing and confession — I am born again of
God's Spirit. This is eternal life, this is having God's
seed born within and thus becoming a son of God by
birth.

The moment God's seed is in a man, that person is
converted, saved, born again. A man can be a natural
man of body and soul one minute, but when he hears
the Word of God to the end of believing, he receives
the faith of Jesus Christ. When that man by his
believing comes to the point of saying, "Jesus is Lord
of my life and I believe God raised Him from the
dead," he is born again of God's Spirit. That person
has instantly changed lords; he is now on the way to
heaven and all hell cannot stop him from going because He is a son of God having Christ in him. He has
eternal life. He is no longer a natural man (simply a
body-and-soul being) because he has received the
spirit from God.

When a child is physically born, all his human potential is in that little package. With nurturing and feeding, the child develops into an adolescent, then into a youth and finally into an adult. The new birth is like that. When a man is born again of God's Spirit, he has Christ in him. Everything that God is in Christ is in the born-again believer. He has the love of God, he has the justification of God, the sanctification, the redemption, the righteousness, the faith of Jesus Christ, the potential power of Jesus Christ. This is what one receives when he accepts the Lord Jesus Christ as his personal Lord and Savior and becomes a son of God.

> I John 3:2:
> Beloved, now are we the sons of God, and it doth not yet appear what we shall be: but we know that, when he shall appear, we shall be like him; for we shall see him as he is.

Now we are the sons of God by way of the spiritual birth, which is Christ in us the hope of glory. As God's children, we are Christ's brethren; for Jesus Christ was God's Son our Savior. The Lord Jesus Christ is our brother.

> Romans 8:17:
> And if children, then heirs; heirs of God, and joint-heirs with Christ ....

Since the Old Testament sons by adoption performed the feats which are recorded in Hebrews 11, how much more we as born-again sons of God and joint-heirs with Christ should manifest courage and power. We have God in Christ within us. No one can separate us from the love of God our Father because we are born again of God's incorruptible seed which is Eternal and which is Life.

CHAPTER SIX

The Third Heaven and Earth

II Corinthians 12:2 has caused considerable confusion in Christian circles. If we have respect for the integrity of God's Word, however, and if we believe that the Word of God is the Will of God and that it means what it says and says what it means, then we will have no difficulty in establishing in our minds the "what and where" of the third heaven. We certainly cannot go by secular literature nor by what denominations have written about this subject, but we must adhere to the Word of God.

II Corinthians 12:1-4:
It is not expedient for me doubtless to glory. I will come to visions and revelations of the Lord.

I knew a man in Christ above fourteen years ago, (whether in the body, I cannot tell; or whether out of the body, I cannot tell: God knoweth;) such an one caught up to the third heaven.

And I knew such a man, (whether in the body, or out of the body, I cannot tell: God knoweth;)

How that he was caught up into paradise, and heard unspeakable words, which it is not lawful for a man to utter.

In order to have an accurate understanding of The Word, let us consider first the words "caught up" of verse two. Whenever we speak or think of the words "caught up," we think of them in terms of height. However, that is not the meaning of the word used in the text; "caught up" would be more clearly translated as "caught away." The same Greek word, *harpazō*, is used in a number of other instances.

John 10:12:
But he that is an hireling, and not the shepherd, whose own the sheep are not, seeth the wolf coming, and leaveth the sheep, and fleeth: and the wolf catcheth them, and scattereth the sheep.

"Catcheth" is the same Greek word that is also translated "caught up," "caught away," "taketh away" or "snatcheth away."

I will give all the usages of this word *harpazō* in the New Testament, so that each student may study the passages and come to his own understanding of it. It is translated as follows: "catcheth," John 10:12; "catcheth away," Matthew 13:19; Acts 8:39; "catch up," II Corinthians 12:2,4; I Thessalonians 4:17; Revelation 12:5; "pluck," John 10:28,29; "pull," Jude 23; and "take by force," Matthew 11:12; John 6:15; Acts 23:10. These could all be translated "catch" or "catch away." In II Corinthians 12:2 and 4 *harpazō* is in the aorist tense denoting a "once and one time only occurrence." Paul was *caught up* to the third heaven, paradise, once and only once. He was given this revelation once and for all.

The Bible speaks of three heavens. These three heavens, however, are not in layers, but rather in sequence — three different periods of time. These are all set forth in II Peter. The first heaven and earth of Genesis 1:1 is spoken of in II Peter 3:6 as "the world that then was."

> II Peter 3:6:
> Whereby the world that then was, being over-flowed with water, perished.

"Being overflowed with water, perished" does not refer to the flood of Noah's time. The word "perished" refers to the "destruction" as recorded in Genesis 1:2. The second heaven and earth is noted in the following verse of II Peter 3.

II Peter 3:7:

But the heavens and the earth, which are now, by the same word are kept in store, reserved unto fire against the day of judgment and perdition of ungodly men.

"The heavens and the earth which are now" is the second heaven and earth, the substance which God put in order after the first creation became "without form and void."

Verse 13 of II Peter 3 tells of the third heaven and earth.

II Peter 3:13:

Nevertheless we, according to his promise, look for new heavens and a new earth, wherein dwelleth righteousness.

"New heavens* and a new earth" is the third heaven and earth. Following are God's comments on the matter dealing with heaven and earth.

We know that sometime, in some way, the first earth became utterly ruined.

Genesis 1:1,2:

In the beginning God created the heaven and the earth.

*Heaven is used in the plural indicating God is Lord over all His creation including the stars, planets and such, plus the earth. In the Greek "heaven," when used in the singular, sets heaven in contrast with earth. In Matthew 6:9 the singular "heaven" is used.

And the earth was [became] without form, and void; and darkness *was* upon the face [faces] of the deep. And the Spirit of God moved upon the face of the waters.

"The heaven and the earth" are the first ones, and they fell into ruin. Then came "the heavens and the earth, which are now." But a day is coming when there will be a new heaven and a new earth, this being the third heaven and earth.

Revelation 21:1:

And I saw a new heaven and a new earth: for the first* [former] heaven and the first [former] earth were passed away; and there was no more sea.†

This is referred to as the third heaven and earth.

Paul was "caught away" by revelation to this, the third heaven, the existence of which is still future. How beautiful and how simple The Word becomes. It is no longer private interpretation or guesswork. Paul was "caught away" to the new heaven and the new earth, the third one; God showed him by revelation exactly what this was all about.

II Corinthians 12:1:

It is not expedient for me doubtless to glory. I will come to visions and revelations of the Lord.

*The Greek word for "first" is translated "before" in John 1:15,30.
†"No more sea," is a Hebraism referring to "no more wavering, confusion, trouble or unrighteousness."

There are four different Greek words used for the word "not" in the Bible. The one used in this verse means "absolutely not." "It is [absolutely] not expedient [necessary] for me doubtless to glory ...." The word "glory" means to "speak authoritatively" of those things of which he has *true* knowledge.

"I will come to visions and revelations of the Lord." The literal translation of this is: "I have had visions regarding the revelation of the Lord."

> Revelation 1:1:
> The Revelation of Jesus Christ, which God gave unto him, to shew unto his servants things which must shortly come to pass; and he sent and signified *it* by his angel unto his servant John.

This book of Revelation is called in its first verse "The Revelation of Jesus Christ." The word "revelation" is the Greek word *apokalupsis*, transliterated "apocalypse" meaning "appearing" or "revelation" of Jesus Christ. This will be His second coming.

> II Corinthians 12:2:
> I knew a man in Christ above [more than] fourteen years ago, (whether in the body, I cannot tell; or whether out of the body, I cannot tell: God knoweth:) such an one caught up to the third heaven.

"Knew" is a unique word, meaning "knew without effort." How could anyone know something without putting forth any effort? The Word says by *revelation* which is received by word of knowledge and word of wisdom.

"I knew a man in Christ ...." The word "in" is the word "remaining within." Paul believed in eternal life, he did not get saved one minute and lost the next minute, and he was walking in fellowship. "I knew [without effort] a man in Christ [remaining in Christ] ...."

These few words "(whether in the body, I cannot tell, or whether out of the body, I cannot tell: God knoweth;)" — are used in the same sense we describe a person who becomes enthusiastic over something. We may say that he is "beside himself" with joy or "out of this world."

> Luke 4:5:
> And the devil, taking him up into an high mountain, shewed unto him all the kingdoms of the world in a moment of time.

"Shewed unto him all the kingdoms of the world in a moment of time" was by *revelation*. The devil could not take Jesus up into a high mountain and show him all the kingdoms of the world physically. This could be done only by revelation.

Ezekiel 40:24:
After that he brought me toward the south, and behold a gate toward the south: and he measured the posts thereof and the arches thereof according to these measures.

"After that he brought me." God "brought" Ezekiel and showed this to him, the same as Paul was "caught away" to the third heaven.

Ezekiel 40:2:
In the visions of God brought he me into the land of Israel, and set me upon a very high mountain ....

God "brought" him and set him on a very high mountain by revelation.

II Corinthians 12:4:
How that he was caught up into paradise, and heard unspeakable words, which it is not lawful for a man to utter.

"Caught up" of II Corinthians 12:2 is the same as "caught up" of verse four. Both literally mean "caught away."

The word "into" is a precise preposition. It is not the same preposition as the one given at the end of verse 2 of II Corinthians 12. Not only was Paul "caught away" to the third heaven, but also "caught away" into paradise. "To" is the Greek word *eis*, which means a motion toward an object with the intent of reaching the object. The Word leaves us breathless in its accuracy!

"How that he was caught away into paradise." Paradise is a heaven on earth. In the heaven and earth in Genesis 2, God was with man and could talk to man. There was no sickness, no sin and no death; that was paradise. Paradise is never any other place than upon earth. The unorthodox teaching we have had is that paradise is an intermediate state, a purgatory. This is total error. The Word of God says it is a place on earth.

The Septuagint uses the word "*paradosia*," paradise, for Eden in all the following passages: Genesis 2:8,10,15; 3:23,24; 4:16; Isaiah 51:3; Ezekiel 28:13; 31:9,16,18; 36:35; Joel 2:3.

We find "paradise" in Genesis 2, but we never read about "paradise" again until Revelation 21, when there is a new heaven and a new earth.

Returning to verse 4 of II Corinthians 12 we read: "How that he was caught up into paradise, and heard unspeakable words ...." Why is the word "unspeakable" used? The reason was not that Paul could not have used words in his own vocabulary to express what God had shown him,* but God knew that the time of revelation in writing was not yet. The Apostle John, not Paul, was to write this.

> Revelation 1:1:
> ... and he sent and signified *it* by his angel unto his servant John.

There are two different Greek words used for "word" in the Bible. One is *logos*,† the other is *rhēma*. The usage in II Corinthians 12:4 is *rhēma*, meaning "sentences." Paul was caught away into paradise and heard unspeakable, not to be disclosed, sentences. God showed him, by revelation, many things that were still future, but which were not to be spoken nor written by Paul, "... which it is not lawful [which it is not permitted] for a man to utter," to speak forth so someone else could hear.

God caught Paul away to the period of time of the third earth. Why did He do this? The answer is given in the context of II Corinthians 11 and 12. In these chapters, Paul was talking about his "thorn in the flesh," people who were inspired by Satan to make

---

*II Peter 1:21: "For the prophecy came not in old time by the will of man: but holy men of God spake *as they were* moved by the Holy Ghost."

†*Logos* is "The Word" which is God.

his life miserable. Paul had suffered Satanic persecution. Three times Paul had prayed to the Father to remove Satan's attack, and then the Father gave him a "free trip." By revelation, God took Paul to the third heaven and the third earth, "wherein dwelleth righteousness." God showed him all these things which were "unspeakable."

Now we can understand why Paul spoke as he did in II Corinthians 12.

II Corinthians 12:5,6:
Of such an one will I glory: yet of myself I will not glory, but in mine infirmities.

For though I would desire to glory, I shall not be a fool; for I will say the truth: but *now* I forbear, lest any man should think of me above that which he seeth me *to be,* or *that* he heareth of me.

"Of such an one will I glory ..." because God, by revelation (word of knowledge and word of wisdom) showed Paul tremendous events.

II Corinthians 12:10:
Therefore I take pleasure in infirmities, in reproaches, in necessities, in persecutions, in distresses for Christ's sake: for when I am weak, then am I strong.

Here in the midst of this heaven and earth which are *now,* where we suffer persecution, we labor not in vain, but we look for His return and the new heaven and the new earth, wherein dwelleth righteousness.

> Romans 8:18:
> For I reckon that the sufferings of this present time *are* not worthy *to be compared* with the glory which shall be revealed in us.

The persecutions which we suffer now are short compared to the joys of the new heaven and the new earth, wherein dwelleth righteousness, and of which there shall be no end.

In a discussion of paradise we must also consider the words of Jesus to the malefactor as He was hanging on the cross.

> Luke 23:42,43:
> And he [the malefactor] said unto Jesus, Lord, remember me when thou comest into thy kingdom.
>
> And Jesus said unto him, Verily I say unto thee, To day shalt thou be with me in paradise.

Remembering that paradise is a place on earth, we know that paradise did not exist on the day the malefactor died. The malefactor requested something in the future. "Kingdom" is used synonymously with "paradise" and the "third heaven and earth." The Bible says that the malefactor was a believing Israelite and believers of Israel will occupy paradise. Jesus promised the malefactor something on the day of the crucifixion which was all Jesus could promise to him, because the malefactor was *of Israel.* Jesus did not say to him, "Verily, verily I say unto thee, Today thou shalt go to heaven." No, if Jesus had meant heaven, He would have said heaven. Jesus said "paradise" because He meant "paradise," which is referring to a place on earth in the future.

Jesus never went to heaven nor paradise (as some erroneously call it) when He died. He went into the grave.* The third day God raised Jesus, not from paradise nor heaven, but from the grave. The malefactor's request was "Lord, remember me when thou comest [future tense] into thy kingdom" and the coming into His own kingdom is not heaven and not paradise, but His kingdom which is yet future.†

According to John 14:3 Jesus said He would take His followers to Himself at some future time. The

*I Corinthians 15:3b,4: "... how that Christ died for our sins according to the scriptures; And that he was buried, and that he rose again the third day according to the scriptures."
Luke 24:46: "And said unto them, Thus it is written, and thus it behoved Christ to suffer, and to rise from the dead the third day."
†See Luke 23:42, I Corinthians 15:24 and Revelation 11:15.

King James Version has a comma after the word "thee" in Luke 23:43, but this comma must be deleted. Leaving the comma where the King James Version has it causes the Bible to be inaccurate. Paradise is *not* now; therefore, Jesus said to the malefactor, "Verily I say unto thee today, thou shalt be [future tense] with me in paradise."

> I Thessalonians 4:16,17:
> For the Lord himself shall descend from heaven with a shout, with the voice of the archangel, and with the trump of God: and the dead in Christ shall rise first:
>
> Then we which are alive *and* remain shall be caught up together with them in the clouds, to meet the Lord in the air: and so shall we ever be with the Lord.

We can see from these Scriptures that this future time for taking the Church to dwell with Christ is at the gathering together unto Him. The gathering together takes place before the penitent malefactor will have been remembered by the Lord and will have been given a place in paradise because he was of the house of Israel. This is the accuracy of God's Word.

In the parable of the rich man and Lazarus in Luke 16:19-31, the rich man, who had died, made the request for Lazarus to be sent to his Father's house. Lazarus was to warn the rich man's brethren concerning his situation.

Luke 16:29-31:
Abraham saith unto him, They have Moses and the prophets; let them hear them.

And he said, Nay, father Abraham: but if one went unto them from the dead, they will repent.

And he said unto him, If they hear not Moses and the prophets, neither will they be persuaded, though one rose from the dead.

This is a plain statement that Lazarus was dead and in the grave. Before he could warn others, he must rise from the dead, not return from paradise or heaven.

The third heaven and earth is spoken of in Revelation.

Revelation 2:7:
He that hath an ear, let him hear what the Spirit saith unto the churches; To him that overcometh will I give to eat of the tree of life, which is in the midst of the paradise [Eden] of God.

Isaiah 65:17:
For, behold, I create new heavens and a new
earth: and the former shall not be remembered,
nor come into mind.

God said in Isaiah that He is going to create "new
heavens and a new earth" and this former one, the
one we are living in now, "shall not be remembered."
There will be no memory of it; for in the new heaven
and new earth dwells only righteousness. In the
present heavens and earth, the only righteousness is
the spirit from God in our lives and the manifestation
of that spirit.

Isaiah 51:16:
And I have put my words in thy mouth, and I
have covered thee in the shadow of mine hand,
that I may plant the heavens, and lay the foun-
dations of the earth, and say unto Zion, Thou
art my people.

In context, this is the revelation to Isaiah regarding
the new heavens and the new earth.

Isaiah 66:22:
For as the new heavens and the new earth,
which I will make, shall remain before me, saith
the Lord, so shall your seed and your name
remain.

Isaiah 51:3:

For the Lord shall comfort Zion: he will comfort all her waste places; and he will make her
wilderness like Eden [paradise], and her desert
like the garden of the Lord; joy and gladness
shall be found therein, thanksgiving, and the
voice of melody.

God is going to make the "garden of the Lord"
(the paradise of the Lord) like the paradise recorded
in chapters one and two of Genesis. Isaiah's prophecy
refers to the new heavens and the new earth period.

Ezekiel 28:13:

Thou [Lucifer] hast been in Eden [paradise]
the garden of God; every precious tone *was* thy
covering, the sardius, topaz, and the diamond,
the beryl, the onyx, and the jasper, the sapphire
the emerald, and the carbuncle, and gold: the
workmanship of thy tabrets and of thy pipes are
prepared in thee in the day that thou wast
created.

"Thou," Lucifer, was in the "garden of God." He
was in Eden, the *paradosia,* paradise of God. It was in
Eden that Lucifer did his mischief recorded in
Genesis 3.

Ezekiel 31:8,9:

The cedars in the garden of God could not
hide him: the fir trees were not like his boughs,

and the chestnut trees were not like his branches; nor any tree in the garden of God was like unto him in his beauty.

I have made him fair by the multitude of his branches: so that all the trees of Eden [paradise] that *were* in the garden of God, envied him.

Here is the same usage. The "garden of God," "Eden" and "paradise" are all the same usage.

The preceding has set forth a detailed, word-by-word study of II Corinthians 12:1-11. The following is a literal translation of it according to usage and meaning and gives the exact thought content.

II Corinthians 12:1-11:

It is absolutely not expedient for me to speak of those things of which I have true revealed knowledge.

I have had visions regarding the revelation of the Lord, without effort on my part, because of my remaining position in Christ. More than fourteen years ago I was "beside myself" with joy because I was caught away, in time, to the third heaven. I was caught away as far as paradise where I heard, by revelation, words which are not permitted for me to speak.

Of this time of the third heaven I have real knowledge, yet of my own self I could not have such real knowledge; but, only of those things blocking me from being able to do what I want to do and which should be done. Even if I desired to speak forth this revealed knowledge, it would be unwise; so I abstain from doing so that no one may esteem me beyond what he really sees or hears me to be.

And lest I seem to lift myself above others, due to the abundance of this revelation, there was given to me a thorn in the flesh, the messenger of Satan who "hit" me with all his strength.

Because of Satan's attacks upon me, I besought the Lord three times that He might remove these attacks.

And the Lord said to me "My divine favor is to be of use to you because my inherent power is consummated in you in action when and where you are hindered."

Most gladly, therefore, will I keep this revealed knowledge to myself, also the effects of Satan's attacks, knowing that the inherent power of Christ is consummated in me.

Therefore, I assert myself in behalf of Christ when Satan attacks me violently by way of physical attacks and mental anguish; for when Satan attacks I assert my power.

I have not expressed myself to you regarding my real knowledge of Christ which is in me, for you made it impossible for me to be free to do so.*

I should have been expressing myself to you and you should have represented me worthy to others, for in nothing have I fallen behind of the most eminent apostles.

These are all the references in the Bible regarding the subject of the three heavens and earths. We now understand that the first heaven and the first earth is the one of Genesis 1:1, the second is the one which now exists and the third heaven and earth is the one that is still future -- "the new heavens and the new earth wherein dwelleth righteousness."

*The Corinthian Christians were not spiritually able to receive and understand the deeper spiritual revelation God had given to Paul.

Part II

Points of View

Part II

Points of View

In our earthly life all of us are aware that viewpoints on a given situation vary with each observer. The eye of each beholder sees and then interprets an event according to values, preconceived ideas and previous experiences. Thus each person's point of view differs at least somewhat from another person's.

The Bible shows us that this is not only true of humans. God's viewpoint, however, is omniscient. And in the two chapters which follow, "Viewpoints: God's — Man's" and "Of Human Sacrifice," we study how man interprets a situation and then how God sees the same situation. The lives of King Saul and King Jehoshaphat are researched in the first chapter, and the sacrifice of Isaac by Abraham in the second chapter. When we understand "Points of View," our minds are enlightened and comforted.

CHAPTER SEVEN

Viewpoints: God's -- Man's

In studying the books of I and II Samuel, I and II
Kings and I and II Chronicles, one occasionally finds
what seems to be contradictory accounts of the same
man or incident. Careful research of these comparable
records soon discloses a shift of viewpoint from one
account to its counterpart in another Old Testament
book. The books of Samuel and Kings are written
from a human viewpoint, man's point of view. The
books of Chronicles, on the other hand, are written
from God's point of view, from the vantage point of
spiritual power. Man's point of view will simplify life
to apparent, overt actions; but God, understanding
the spiritual forces at work in the world, goes beneath
the surface and points out the spiritual aspects which
bring about man's destiny.

The accounts of two kings, Saul and Jehoshaphat,
are clear examples of the changes of viewpoint from
man's analysis to God's over-all view. Records of the

Points of View

death of Saul are found in I Samuel 31, from man's
viewpoint, and in I Chronicles 10, from God's viewpoint.

At the end of his life, Saul is once more battling
the Philistines.

> I Samuel 31:1-6:
> Now the Philistines fought against Israel: and
> the men of Israel fled from before the Philis-
> tines, and fell down slain in mount Gilboa.
>
> And the Philistines followed hard upon Saul and
> upon his sons; and the Philistines slew Jonathan,
> and Abinadab, and Malchishua, Saul's sons.
>
> And the battle went sore against Saul, and the
> archers hit him; and he was sore wounded of the
> archers.
>
> Then said Saul unto his armourbearer, Draw thy
> sword, and thrust me through therewith; lest
> these uncircumcised come and thrust me
> through, and abuse me. But his armourbearer
> would not; for he was sore afraid. Therefore
> Saul took a sword, and fell upon it.
>
> And when his armourbearer saw that Saul was
> dead, he fell likewise upon his sword, and died
> with him.

110

So Saul died, and his three sons, and his armour-bearer, and all his men, that same day together.

The record in Samuel makes Saul's death seem like an act of stress brought on by the defeat of battle. Chronicles shows the spiritual forces which brought on Saul's wretched end.

> I Chronicles 10:13,14:
> So Saul died for his transgression which he committed against the Lord, *even* against the word of the Lord, which he kept not, and also for asking *counsel of one that had* a familiar spirit, to inquire *of it;*
>
> And inquired not of the Lord: therefore he slew him, and turned the kingdom unto David the son of Jesse.

From the record in Samuel we learned that the Philistines shot Saul with an arrow, and then Saul impaled himself on his own sword. According to Chronicles, the Lord slew him. How does one harmonize these apparent discrepancies?

Remember, the record in Samuel is from man's point of view: God looked beyond the arrow and the sword. From God's point of view, Saul died because of his transgressions which included his visit to the sensitive to gain information.

Saul disobeyed God's law, and because of his own disobedience killed himself or was killed. God didn't literally take Saul's life. I Chronicles 10:14 doesn't mean that. There is a spiritual law founded by God. Picture the law as a cement wall. When a person runs into it, he hurts himself. Saul knew that God's number one law said man should not pay tribute to idols or other gods: "Thou shalt have no other gods before me." Later on Jesus Christ set forth the commandment: "Thou shalt love the Lord thy God with all thy heart, and with all thy soul, and with all thy strength and with all thy mind" (Luke 10:27). God will bear many acts of unrighteousness from His people, but He will not tolerate the worshipping of other gods.

Saul knew God's commandment, but nevertheless he willfully broke it. Saul, disobeying the true God, began playing with spiritualistic power by having the woman of Endor trying to conjure up the dead Samuel. By this act, Saul rushed head-first against the immovable wall of the law, and thus brought destruction to himself. From the senses' vantage point, Saul died because of battle wounds and self-inflicted impaling. From the spiritual point of view Saul died because he disobeyed the most important law of God.

Another example of the two viewpoints, human and spiritual, is found in the account of Jehoshaphat,

112

king of Judah, in I Kings 22 and II Chronicles 20. Instead of studying just the varied viewpoints of one event in Jehoshaphat's life, let us look at the background leading up to this event. The biography of Jehoshaphat is a record of a frail, though sometimes great, human being, and an example of God's indulgence and faithfulness to His own.

II Chronicles 17:1:
And Jehoshaphat his [Asa's] son reigned in his stead, and strengthened himself against Israel.

Jehoshaphat strengthened himself against Israel, which nation at that time was very wicked and ungodly. Jeroboam of Israel had been a wicked king setting up many high places (temples on hills) to worship pagan gods. And Ahab, Jeroboam's son, continued his father's idolatrous practices when he succeeded his father to the throne of Israel. Jeroboam suffered the loss of his captured cities of refuge at the hand of the king of Judah, Abijah. Abijah's son, Asa, followed in the footsteps of his father and kept the people of Judah from worshipping pagan gods. And Jehoshaphat, the son of Asa, "strengthened himself against Israel," meaning that Jehoshaphat continued the practice of Abijah, his grandfather and Asa, his father, and further ordered all idolatry, including all high places in the land, to be destroyed.

113

In contrast to Jehoshaphat, King Ahab of Israel, following the pattern of his father Jeroboam, continued constructing many high places for pagan worship with all kinds of idols therein.

The king of Israel and the king of Judah were spiritual opposites, and it temporarily appeared that they were going to remain very distant from each other. Not only did Jehoshaphat strengthen himself against Israel, but he also "placed forces in the fenced cities of Judah," the cities of refuge which had been captured from the wicked father of Ahab. Jehoshaphat did not want Ahab to recapture the fenced cities of Judah which were designed to harbor people who accidentally killed or injured a person. God was pleased with the actions of Jehoshaphat, and thus God established an alliance with Jehoshaphat. An alliance with God is always an asset.

II Chronicles 17:3-6, 9-12:
And the Lord was with Jehoshaphat, because he walked in the first ways of his father David, and sought not unto Baalim;

But sought to the *Lord* God of his father, and walked in his commandments, and not after the doings of Israel.

Therefore the Lord established the kingdom in his hand; and all Judah brought to Jehoshaphat presents; and he had riches and honour in abundance.

And his heart was lifted up in the ways of the Lord: moreover he took away the high places and groves out of Judah.

And they [priests] taught in Judah, and *had* the book of the law of the Lord with them, and went about throughout all the cities of Judah, and taught the people [Jehoshaphat had the Word of God taught to the people of Judah].

And the fear of the Lord fell upon all the kingdoms of the lands that *were* round about Judah, so that they made no war against Jehoshaphat.

Also *some* of the Philistines brought Jehoshaphat presents, and tribute silver; and the Arabians brought him flocks, seven thousand and seven hundred rams, and seven thousand and seven hundred he goats.

And Jehoshaphat waxed great exceedingly; and he built in Judah castles, and cities of store.

115

Jehoshaphat not only waxed great, he waxed great *exceedingly*. Why? Because of God's alliance with him.

> II Chronicles 18:1:
> Now Jehoshaphat had riches and honour in abundance, and joined affinity with Ahab.

Jehoshaphat, after strengthening himself against Israel, had great success in wealth and prestige. However, as time went on, Jehoshaphat developed a pride in his success which gave him a false sense of security and a feeling of superiority. This change in Jehoshaphat's life rerouted his future. Jehoshaphat overestimated his own ability, and instead of keeping his alliance singularly with God, he aligned himself with the idolatrous king of Israel, Ahab, against whom he had formerly set up a defense. The alliance between Jehoshaphat and Ahab came in the form of an interfamily marriage. Jehoshaphat had his oldest son, Jehoram, marry Ahab's daughter.

When Jehoshaphat joined affinity with Ahab, did the Lord forsake Jehoshaphat? No. Jehoshaphat forsook the Lord. With the marriage of Jehoshaphat's son to Ahab's daughter, Jehoshaphat was forced by protocol to accept Ahab's hospitality.

116

Before the inter-family marriage took place, Ahab could never have gotten Jehoshaphat to go to the capital city of Israel. But once the marriage occurred, Jehoshaphat, the father-in-law, could hardly refuse the overtures of Ahab.

> II Chronicles 18:2:
> And after *certain* years he [Jehoshaphat] went down to Ahab to Samaria [capital of Israel]. And Ahab killed sheep and oxen for him in abundance, and for the people that *he had* with him, and persuaded him to go up *with him* to Ramoth-gilead.

Ramoth-gilead was a city of refuge which originally belonged to Israel but which the Syrians had captured.

> Verses 3 and 4:
> And Ahab king of Israel said unto Jehoshaphat king of Judah, Wilt thou go [to fight] with me to Ramoth-gilead? And he [Jehoshaphat] answered him, I *am* as thou *art,* and my people as thy people; and *we will be* with thee in the war.
>
> And Jehoshaphat said unto the king of Israel, Inquire, I pray thee, at the word of the Lord to day.

117

Although Jehoshaphat had an alliance with Ahab, still within himself he sensed that there was something wrong in trying to recapture Ramoth-gilead. Even though Ahab had made up his mind to recapture Ramoth-gilead and Jehoshaphat had given his word that he would go with Ahab, Jehoshaphat knew that all was not right. So before marching off to battle, Jehoshaphat requested that Ahab ask the Lord what He thought of their plan. This sounds a little bit like all of us. We decide what we want to do, and then we ask God for His stamp of approval.

> Verses 5 and 6:
> Therefore the king of Israel gathered together of prophets four hundred men, and said unto them, Shall we go to Ramoth-gilead to battle, or shall I forbear? And they [the four hundred prophets] said, Go up; for God will deliver *it* into the king's hand.
>
> But Jehoshaphat said [to Ahab], *Is there* not here a prophet of the Lord besides [these four hundred], that we might inquire of him?

Jehoshaphat said to Ahab, "Is there possibly another prophet of the Lord that we could ask about our plans? I'm still not satisfied that we're doing the right thing." Four hundred so-called prophets had already told Ahab and Jehoshaphat that their plan

118

was approved, but Jehoshaphat wanted to hold out for the confirmation from one more.

Verses 7–26:
And the king of Israel said unto Jehoshaphat, *There is* yet one man, by whom we may inquire of the Lord: but I hate him; for he never prophesied [anything] good unto me, but always evil: the same *is* Micaiah the son of Imla. And Jehoshaphat said, Let not the king say so.

And the king of Israel called for one *of his* officers, and said, Fetch quickly Micaiah the son of Imla.

And the king of Israel and Jehoshaphat king of Judah sat either of them on his throne, clothed in *their* robes, and they sat in a void place at the entering in of the gate of Samaria; and all the prophets prophesied before them.

And Zedekiah [one of the four hundred] the son of Chenaanah had made him horns of iron, and said, Thus saith the Lord, With these thou shalt push Syria until they be consumed.

119

And all the prophets prophesied so, saying, Go up to Ramoth-gilead, and prosper: for the Lord shall deliver *it* into the hand of the king.

And the messenger that went to call Micaiah spake to him, saying, Behold, the words of the prophets [the four hundred who have already spoken] *declare* good to the king with one assent; let thy word therefore, I pray thee, be like one of theirs, and [for once in your life] speak thou good.

And Micaiah said, *As* the Lord liveth, even what my God saith, that will I speak.

And when he [Micaiah] was come to the king, the king said unto him, Micaiah, shall we go to Ramoth-gilead to battle, or shall I forbear? And he [Micaiah] said, Go ye up, and prosper, and they shall be delivered into your hand.

And the king [Jehoshaphat] said to him, How many times shall I adjure thee that thou say nothing but the truth to me in the name of the Lord?

Then he [Micaiah] said, I did see all Israel scattered upon the mountains, as sheep that have no shepherd: and the Lord said, These have no master; let them return *therefore* every man to his house in peace.

And the king of Israel said to Jehoshaphat, Did I not tell thee *that* he would not prophesy good unto me, but evil?

Again he [Micaiah] said, Therefore hear the word of the Lord; I saw the Lord sitting upon his throne, and all the host of heaven standing on his right hand and *on* his left.

And the Lord said, Who shall entice Ahab king of Israel, that he may go up and fall at Ramoth-gilead? And one spake saying after this manner, and another saying after that manner.

Then there came out a spirit, and stood before the Lord, and said, I will entice him. And the Lord said unto him, Wherewith?

And he [the spirit] said, I will go out, and be a lying spirit in the mouth of all his prophets [all four hundred]. And *the Lord* said, Thou shalt entice *him*, and thou shalt also prevail: go out, and do *even* so.

Now therefore, behold, the Lord hath put a lying spirit in the mouth of these thy prophets, and the Lord hath spoken evil against thee.

Then Zedekiah the son of Chenaanah came near, and smote Micaiah upon his cheek [To touch a man on the cheek is to disgrace him. When Jesus was smote on the cheek before being brought out for His crucifixion, Jesus was terribly disgraced.], and said, Which way went the Spirit of the Lord from me to speak unto thee?

And Micaiah said, Behold, thou [Zedekiah] shalt see on that day when thou shalt go into an inner chamber to hide thyself.

Then the king of Israel said, Take ye Micaiah, and carry him back to Amon the governor of the city, and to Joash the king's son;

And say, Thus saith the king [Ahab], Put this *fellow* in the prison, and feed him with bread of affliction and with water of affliction, until I return in peace.

What a dilemma for Jehoshaphat! After his alliance with Ahab, he was asked by Ahab to go up to Ramoth-gilead and fight the Syrians. Jehoshaphat sensed that something was amiss, even after the favorable prophecies of the four hundred prophets. Jehoshaphat recognized Micaiah as the true prophet of God. He knew that the other four hundred were false prophets, counterfeits, crystal ball gazers, sensitives and those in E.S.P. Having committed himself to Ahab, Jehoshaphat must have been deeply hurt when Ahab had the true prophet imprisoned and fed bread and water of affliction.

Verses 27 and 28:
And Micaiah said, If thou certainly return in peace, *then* hath not the Lord spoken by me. And he [Micaiah] said, Hearken, all ye people.

So the king of Israel and Jehoshaphat the king of Judah went up to Ramoth-gilead.

Ahab bullheadedly proceeded with his plans — after all, the odds were four hundred to one.

Verse 29:
And the king of Israel said unto Jehoshaphat, I will disguise myself, and will go to the battle; but put thou [Jehoshaphat] on thy robes. So the king of Israel disguised himself; and they went to the battle.

This action is described from God's point of view. Note what is happening in the camp of the Syrians from this omniscient vantage point.

Verse 30:
Now the king of Syria had commanded the

123

captains of the chariots that *were* with him,
saying, Fight ye not with small or great, save
only with the king of Israel.

The Syrian king made it clear to his military men
that he didn't want a great deal of blood shed; all he
wanted was the death of the king of Israel.

Verse 31:
And it came to pass, when the captains of the
chariots saw Jehoshaphat, that they said, It *is*
the king of Israel. Therefore they compassed
about him to fight: but Jehoshaphat cried out,
and the Lord helped him; and God moved them
to depart from him.*

Observe the usage of Lord and God in verse 31,
"... the Lord helped him; and God moved them *to
depart* from him." The Hebrew word for "Lord" is
Jehovah, while "God" is the word *Elohim. Jehovah*
helped Jehoshaphat, while *Elohim* moved the Syrians
to depart.

Jehovah was the covenant God. *Jehovah* had a
covenant with Jehoshaphat so that when Jehoshaphat
cried to him, Jehovah helped. But it was God as the

*The Syrians knew only that they were fighting King Ahab and his
forces. So naturally, when they saw Jehoshaphat in his royal garb, they
thought they had spotted their prey.

creator, *Elohim,* who moved the Syrians to depart from Jehoshaphat. Exactly what *Elohim* did to the Syrians is unknown.

Verses 32–34:
For it came to pass, that, when the captains of the chariots perceived that it was not the king of Israel, they turned back again from pursuing him.

And a *certain* man [a Syrian sharp-shooter] drew a bow at a venture, and smote the king of Israel between the joints of the harness: therefore he [Ahab] said to his chariot man, Turn thine hand, that thou mayest carry me out of the host; for I am wounded.

And the battle increased that day: howbeit the king of Israel stayed *himself* up in *his* chariot against the Syrians until the even: and about the time of the sun going down he died.

One prophet had said that Ahab would die while four hundred said that he would be victorious. Micaiah proved to be the true prophet because his prophecy came to pass.*

*Deuteronomy 18:22: "When a prophet speaketh in the name of the Lord, if the thing follow not, nor come to pass, that *is* the thing which the Lord hath not spoken, *but* the prophet hath spoken it presumptuously: thou shalt not be afraid of him."

After the loss in battle at Ramoth-gilead, Jehoshaphat tried to collect himself. He had never known the taste of defeat until he aligned himself with Ahab and ignored the prophecy of Micaiah.

II Chronicles 19:1,2:
And Jehoshaphat the king of Judah returned to his house in peace to Jerusalem.

And Jehu the son of Hanani the seer [the prophet] went out to meet him [Jehoshaphat], and said to king Jehoshaphat, Shouldest thou help the ungodly, and love them that hate the Lord? therefore *is* wrath upon thee from before the Lord.

Many Christians are constantly helping the ungodly who hate the true God. What a message of reproof not only to Jehoshaphat but to all who meddle in the affairs of the ungodly. God overlooks many things in the life of man, but idolatry, paganism, spiritualism, pendant usage and E.S.P. are not overlooked nor forgotten. Jehoshaphat was spared because he had destroyed the groves of Judah where idolatry had been practiced.

After his defeat at Ramoth-gilead, Jehoshaphat set about once more to put his house in order.

126

Verse 4:
And Jehoshaphat dwelt at Jerusalem: and he went out again through the people from Beersheba to mount Ephraim, and brought them back unto the Lord God of their fathers.

II Chronicles 20:30:
So the realm of Jehoshaphat was quiet: for his God gave him rest round about.

But unfortunately for Jehoshaphat, all did not remain restful because Jehoshaphat had not yet learned his lesson in making bad alliances. Later II Chronicles 20 records that Jehoshaphat made another alliance — this time a commercial pact.

II Chronicles 20:35—37:
And after this did Jehoshaphat king of Judah join himself with Ahaziah king of Israel, who did very wickedly [Israel's new king after the death of Ahab was Ahaziah.]:

And he joined himself with him to make ships to go to Tarshish: and they made the ships in Ezion-geber.

Then Eliezer the son of Dodavah of Mareshah prophesied against Jehoshaphat, saying, Because thou hast joined thyself with Ahaziah, the Lord

127

> hath broken thy works. And the ships were broken, that they were not able to go to Tarshish.

Jehoshaphat anticipated the wealth and comfort to be derived from trade with Tarshish, a very rich city. But from God's point of view, the plan was not fit because of Jehoshaphat's alliance with the ungodly Ahaziah, and therefore Jehoshaphat did not succeed. A record of man's point of view of this commercial fiasco is found in I Kings.

> I Kings 22:48:
> Jehoshaphat made ships of Tharshish to go to Ophir for gold: but they went not; for the ships were broken at Ezion-geber.

II Chronicles states that "because thou hast joined thyself with Ahaziah, the Lord hath broken thy works," whereas I Kings attributes the event to natural causes, "for the ships were broken at Ezion-geber."

> Verse 49:
> Then said Ahaziah the son of Ahab unto Jehoshaphat, Let my servants go with thy servants in the ships ....

After the first ships were destroyed, the men built

more ships to go again. Wicked Ahaziah still tried to cajole Jehoshaphat with his commercial plans. Verse 49 ends saying, "... But Jehoshaphat would not."

Jehoshaphat finally had learned his lesson. At a price he learned that an alliance with the ungodly in marriage didn't work; He then learned that an alliance with the ungodly in military exploit didn't work; and lastly, he learned that an alliance with the ungodly in commercial enterprise didn't work.

From man's point of view, it appeared that Jehoshaphat's prosperity and his later defeats came by natural causes. But from God's point of view, success or the lack of it varied directly with Jehoshaphat's obedience to God. When Jehoshaphat accommodated the ungodly, defeat ensued. When he aligned himself with God, prosperity abounded.

Jehoshaphat never worshipped any other god, so his end was not a bloody one. King Saul, however, did break the first commandment in seeking aid from other gods, and in doing so he ran head-first against the law of God and thereby suffered an inglorious death. From man's viewpoint appearances would say that Saul died of a sword sticking through his body; but from God's viewpoint, the spiritual view, Saul died because of disobedience to God.

129

Points of View

Man's point of view is always limited to appearances and a finite overview. God's point of view is comprehensive. The two accounts of Saul in I Samuel and I Chronicles and of Jehoshaphat in II Kings and II Chronicles are not contradictory; they simply contrast the two points of view — God's and man's.

CHAPTER EIGHT

Of Human Sacrifice

Abraham and Isaac

The Biblical record of the offering of Isaac has been a source of confusion and misunderstanding for many years. It is difficult to understand why God apparently asked Abraham to offer Isaac as a burnt offering. If God is the giver of all life, how could He ask Abraham to offer up his only son whom God had promised him? The account of Abraham and Isaac simply has not made sense, and thus critics have constantly wrestled over it.

The record of Abraham and Isaac in Genesis 22:1 begins, "And it came to pass after these things, that God did tempt Abraham ...." The first misconception has stemmed from the word tempt. In Hebrew "tempt" is *bachan*, meaning "to prove." "Tempt"must be incorrect because James 1:13 says that God never tempts.*

Although God never tempts, it is possible for Him to prove man. God proves us as we prove ourselves.

*"Let no man say when he is tempted, I am tempted of God: for God cannot be tempted with evil, neither tempteth he any man."

He gives us His Word and as we walk on it, we are
proved. But God does not tempt us. Only Satan
tempts.

Hebrews 11:17 records, "By faith [believing]
Abraham, when he was tried [proved] offered up
Isaac ...."

> Genesis 22:1,2:
> And it came to pass after these things, that God
> did tempt [prove] Abraham, and said unto him,
> Abraham: and he said, Behold, *here* I *am.*
>
> And he said, Take now thy son, thine only *son*
> Isaac, whom thou lovest, and get thee into the
> land of Moriah; and offer him there for a burnt
> offering upon one of the mountains which I will
> tell thee of.

According to these verses, God told Abraham to
take his son Isaac and offer him for a burnt offering
upon one of the mountains which God would tell
him.

Our whole problem may be that we do not understand what a burnt offering is.* God never asked

*For Biblical research students it is of interest to note that in the
Aramaic Peshitta text the word *ykda*, "burnt," is never used in this
story. The word *alta*, "offering," is used throughout. Thus, could it be
that every sacrifice is an offering, but not every offering a sacrifice?

Abraham to put a fire under Isaac. This idea has come to us because of teachers we have heard, books we have read and pictures we have seen. We have in mind the image of Abraham walking Isaac up the mountain, gathering the sticks, building the altar, tying Isaac and preparing to slay him when suddenly a ram is noticed behind them. This is not the Word of the Lord. What did the Lord tell Abraham to do?

> Genesis 22:2:
> ... Take now thy son, thine only *son* Isaac, whom thou lovest, and get thee into the land of Moriah; and offer him there for a burnt offering upon one of the mountains which I will tell thee of.

This is all that God commanded Abraham to do. So when we understand what a burnt offering is, we will then have the key to the correct understanding of this verse.

To most of us a burnt offering concerns burning something with fire. But in Eastern custom a burnt offering does not indicate the presence of fire. When speaking of people as being a burnt offering, it did not mean sacrifice by fire. *A burnt offering was a total, unreserved commitment of self to God.* Let us note carefully this truth so plainly taught in the record in Judges 11 of Jephthah who gave his daughter as a burnt offering.

133

Judges 11:30–40:

And Jephthah vowed a vow unto the Lord, and said, If thou shalt without fail deliver the children of Ammon into mine hands,

Then it shall be, that whatsoever cometh forth of the doors of my house to meet me, when I return in peace from the children of Ammon, shall surely be the Lord's and I will offer it up for a burnt offering [Carefully notice Jephthah's promise.].

So Jephthah passed over unto the children of Ammon to fight against them; and the Lord delivered them [the children of Ammon] into his hands.

And he smote them ....

And Jephthah came to Mizpeh unto his house, and, behold, his daughter came out to meet him with timbrels and with dances: and she *was his* only child; beside her he had neither son nor daughter.

And it came to pass, when he saw her, that he rent his clothes, and said, Alas, my daughter! thou hast brought me very low, and thou art one of them that trouble me: for I have opened my mouth unto the Lord, and I cannot go back.

And she said unto him, My father, *if* thou hast opened thy mouth unto the Lord, do to me according to that which hath proceeded out of thy mouth; forasmuch as the Lord hath taken vengeance for thee of thine enemies, *even* of the children of Ammon.

And she said unto her father, Let this thing be done for me: let me alone two months, that I may go up and down upon the mountains, and bewail my virginity, I and my fellows.

And he said, Go. And he sent her away *for* two months: and she went with her companions, and bewailed her virginity upon the mountains.

And it came to pass at the end of two months, that she returned unto her father, who did with her *according* to his vow which he had vowed: and she knew no man. And it was a custom in Israel,

That the daughters of Israel went yearly to lament [visit*] the daughter of Jephthah the Gileadite four days in a year.

Eastern custom teaches us that an unmarried

*King James has the marginal note "talk with." Young's Concordance says "to give praise."

135

maiden is a disgrace not only to the girl herself but also to the family. An unwed daughter indicates that a curse of God is on the family. Often such parents give these maidens as servants to serve at the temples for the rest of their lives. But before the young lady is committed, the maiden vacations in the mountains with relatives and a few close friends and together they have consecration ceremonies for two months, bewailing her virginity — that is, lamenting the fact she did not marry and produce offspring. Then the maiden bids farewell to all her relatives and friends. Once the girl enters into the service of the temple, she cannot be released to go back to her friends, relatives nor parents.

Jephthah gave his daughter permission to go to the mountains for two months. When she came back, her father took her to the temple. There she followed the ceremony all such girls go through. Her head was shaved at the door of the temple and she put on a long robe. She then remained in the temple the rest of her life. During special times each year, people would go and praise her, talk with her and compliment her for obeying her father's will. This account of Jephthah's daughter shows that a burnt offering means that she was living in the temple serving God.

Jephthah had promised God that whatever first came out of the doors of his house to meet him when he returned from battle he would give as a burnt offering. Having no other son or daughter, this child was the only hope of perpetuating Jephthah's family line. The total commitment of his only daughter to God's service was Jephthah's burnt offering. Jephthah felt especially bad because his family line had come to an end.

Just as Jephthah's daughter was dedicated to temple service for her lifetime, so Isaac was totally dedicated and consecrated to the commitment for all Israel believers for all ages as God's people. All Israel was called in Isaac.*

Now let us go back and carefully examine God's command to Abraham. God did not say that Abraham should take wood with him to start a fire. God told Abraham to take Isaac to a mountain and to offer him. Then we read that Abraham prepared himself with all those other things. This shows us that Abraham deliberately went beyond God's commandment.

Genesis 22:3:
And Abraham rose up early in the morning, and saddled his ass, and took two of his young men

---

*Hebrews 11:17,18: "By faith Abraham, when he was tried, offered up Isaac: and he that had received the promises offered up his only begotten *son*, Of whom it was said, That in Isaac shall thy seed be called."

> with him, and Isaac his son, and clave the wood
> for the burnt offering ....

This is the first place we get the idea that Abraham was going to burn Isaac. God's revelation was one thing; Abraham's sense-knowledge was something different.

As you recall, God had revealed long before that He was going to give Abraham a son by Sarah; but Abraham did not believe this until he was old. In the meantime, he took Hagar as his wife and Ishmael was born. Abraham did this by his sense-knowledge. God did keep his promise and Isaac was born to Sarah in her old age. Abraham again acted by his erring sense-knowledge regarding God's commandment concerning the offering of Isaac. Abraham lived near the Canaanites and had seen them burn human sacrifices to their gods. So when God said to Abraham, "Take him and give him as a burnt offering," Abraham immediately injected his own ideas and thought, "Well, that means I'd better take the wood along."

> Genesis 22:3–6:
> ... and rose up, and went unto the place of which God had told him.

> Then on the third day Abraham lifted up his eyes, and saw the place afar off.

And Abraham said unto his young men, Abide ye here with the ass; and I and the lad will go yonder and worship, and come again to you.

And Abraham took the wood of the burnt offering, and laid *it* upon Isaac his son; and he took the fire in his hand, and a knife; and they went both of them together.

Isaac was not just five or six years old at this time. He was a grown adult, age thirty.

Verses 7–9:
And Isaac spake unto Abraham his father, and said, My father: and he said, Here *am* I, my son. And he said, Behold the fire and the wood: but where *is* the lamb for a burnt offering?

And Abraham said, My son, God will provide himself a lamb for a burnt offering: so they went both of them together.

And they came to the place which God had told him of; and Abraham built an altar there, and laid the wood in order, and bound Isaac his son, and laid him on the altar upon the wood.

The Scriptures do not say that God told Abraham to build an altar nor to lay wood on the altar nor to bind Isaac and lay him on the altar. God had told Abraham what to do, but Abraham was the one who thought of a literal burning. He was using his own imagination, influenced by the actions of his unbelieving neighbors, and interjecting his own ideas.

> Verse 10:
> And Abraham stretched forth his hand, and took the knife to slay his son.

Look how really wrong Abraham was.

> Verses 11,12:
> And the angel of the Lord called unto him out of heaven, and said, Abraham, Abraham: and he said, Here *am* I.
>
> And he said, Lay not thine hand upon the lad ....

Had this been God's will, as Abraham thought it was, there never would have been an angel needed to suddenly terminate the action because God cannot contradict Himself, He cannot change His will. It was not God's will to literally burn and kill the young man. This was Abraham's idea. Yet, even though Abraham went beyond God's request and was wrong in so doing, he proved his utter willingness to relinquish his son. Therefore the angel of the Lord could make the following declaration in Genesis 22:12, not because Abraham went beyond God's request, but because he was committed to total relinquishment of his son.

> Genesis 22:12:
> ... for now I know that thou fearest [has awe or reverence for] God, seeing thou hast not withheld thy son, thine only *son* from me.

Paul wrote concerning sacrifice in the book of Romans to us who are in the Church age.

> Romans 12:1,2:
> I beseech you therefore, brethren, by the mercies of God, that ye present [yield] your bodies a living sacrifice, holy, acceptable unto God, *which is* your reasonable service.
>
> And be not conformed to this world: but be ye transformed by the renewing of your mind, that ye may prove what *is* that good, and acceptable, and perfect, will of God.

What good are we to God as dead sacrifices? He needs us as living, active sons to be faithful and carry out this work, totally committed to Him until death. By living according to God's Word, we are proved by Him and are "burnt offerings."

Part III

The Credentials
of Jesus Christ

Part III

The Credentials of Jesus Christ

In order for Jesus Christ to qualify as our Savior, He had to have the proper credentials. "The Genealogy of Jesus Christ" establishes Jesus' line back to King David. "The Conception of Jesus Christ" shows that Jesus was the only-begotten Son of God yet with a human mother. And when looking at Jesus' human relatives, the final chapter, "The Lord's Brethren," examines what the Bible says about Mary's having other children besides Jesus.

To fulfill the law, Jesus had to have a specific pedigree. These are critical studies in maintaining *The Word's Way* and in keeping the law and order of God.

CHAPTER NINE

The Genealogy of Jesus Christ

The record of the birth of Christ is clearly given in the Word of God.

Matthew 1:1:
The book of the generation of Jesus Christ, the son of David, the son of Abraham.

The word "generation" is "offspring" as a part of a family tree. Jesus was the offspring of David, the son of Abraham,* the royal line of Mary. The record in Matthew gives the genealogy of Mary's forefathers.

The legality of the claims for Jesus Christ are confirmed in Matthew because of His mother's bloodline. Mary had to be a direct descendant of the House of David or Christ's claims fail on legal grounds. The record of Matthew 1:1 has to be the family tree of

*Was Abraham a Jew? No. He wasn't a Hebrew either. He was Gentile. The classifications as Hebrews and Judeans came at a much later time.

145

The Credentials of Jesus Christ

Mary's side, she being the only human parent of Jesus Christ.

At the close of the record of Joseph and Mary, Matthew gives an explanation.

> Matthew 1:22,23:
> Now all this was done, that it might be fulfilled which was spoken of the Lord by the prophet [Isaiah], saying,
>
> Behold, a virgin shall be with child ....

Matthew very carefully records the genealogy of Jesus Christ, the son of Mary. "The book of the generation of Jesus Christ." Matthew 1:1–17. (The ancestral line of Mary, the mother of Jesus.)

Abraham to David (14 generations)

1.	Abraham	8.	Aminadab
2.	Isaac	9.	Naasson
3.	Jacob	10.	Salmon
4.	Judas	11.	Booz
5.	Phares	12.	Obed
6.	Esrom	13.	Jesse
7.	Aram	14.	David (the King)

146

David to Carrying away to Babylon
(14 generations)

1.	Solomon	8.	Joatham
2.	Roboam	9.	Achaz
3.	Abia	10.	Ezekias
4.	Asa	11.	Manasses
5.	Josaphat	12.	Amon
6.	Joram	13.	Josias
7.	Ozias	14.	Jechonias

Carrying away to Babylon until Christ
(14 generations)

1.	Salathiel (born after carrying away)	8.	Eliud
2.	Zorobabel	9.	Eleazar
3.	Abiud	10.	Matthan
4.	Eliakim	11.	Jacob
5.	Azor	12.	Joseph (father of Mary)
6.	Sadoc	13.	Mary
7.	Achim	14.	Jesus

Matthew cannot be giving the genealogy of Joseph, the husband of Mary, which theologians have maintained throughout the years, when this Gospel states so clearly that Jesus was conceived by the Holy Spirit.*

> Matthew 1:16:
> And Jacob begat Joseph the husband of Mary ....

This translation in Matthew 1:16 giving Joseph as the husband of Mary is an error, not on the part of the original writer, Matthew, but the subsequent translators. When we examine the records of Matthew in detail, it is evident that God placed a safeguard to enable us to avoid such a misunderstanding. Matthew numbered the genealogical lineage of Jesus Christ and divided it into three groups of 14 generations. This is the safeguard.

> Matthew 1:17:
> So all the generations from Abraham to David *are* fourteen generations; and from David until the carrying away into Babylon *are* fourteen generations; and from the carrying away into Babylon unto Christ *are* fourteen generations.

Counting carefully in the record of the Gospel of Matthew, we note that the first two groupings each contain fourteen generations, but the third group would have only thirteen generations if Joseph were the husband of Mary. Furthermore, Luke 3:23 de-

---

*Matthew 1:20: "But while he thought on these things, behold, the angel of the Lord appeared unto him in a dream, saying, Joseph, thou son of David, fear not to take unto thee Mary thy wife: for that which is conceived in her is of the Holy Ghost."

clares the father of Joseph to be Heli, while Matthew 1:16 declares the father of Joseph to be Jacob. How do you reconcile the apparent discrepancy? The two Josephs certainly cannot be the same if the Word of God is the Will of God and means what it says and says what it means.

Comparing the records as given by Matthew and Luke, it is only logical and reasonable that they must be speaking of two different people named Joseph. The error in Matthew is due to the mistranslation of the Greek word *andra* as "husband," instead of "father." In Matthew 1:16 the Greek word *andra* is from the root word *anēr*. *Anēr* is a male person of full age and stature as opposed to a child or female.

I Corinthians 13:11:
When I was a child, I spake as a child, I understood as a child, I thought as a child: but when I became a man [*anēr*], I put away childish things.

Acts 1:16:
Men [*anēr*] *and* brethren, this scripture must needs have been fulfilled, which the Holy Ghost by the mouth of David spake before concerning Judas, which was guide to them that took Jesus.

I Corinthians 16:13:
Watch ye, stand fast in the faith, quit you like

149

men [anēr], be strong.

I Peter 3:1:
Likewise, ye wives, *be* in subjection to your own
husbands [anēr]; that, if any obey not the word,
they also may without the word be won by the
conversation of the wives.

Acts 17:5:
But the Jews which believed not, moved with
envy, took unto them certain lewd fellows
[anēr] of the baser sort, and gathered a company, and set all the city on an uproar, and
assaulted the house of Jason, and sought to
bring them out to the people.

Acts 7:26:
And the next day he shewed himself unto them
as they strove, and would have set them at one
again, saying, Sirs [anēr], ye are brethren; why
do ye wrong one to another?

Luke 24:19:
And he said unto them, What things? And they
said unto him, Concerning Jesus of Nazareth,
which was a prophet [anēr] mighty in deed and
word before God and all the people.

Acts 3:14:
But ye denied the Holy One and the Just, and

desired a murderer [*anēr*] to be granted unto you.

Anēr is used of an adult male person in various relations where the context must determine its true meaning. As indicated in the above verses the usage of *anēr* in its relationship is as follows: (1) man; (2) husband; (3) fellow; (4) sir; (5) a man as a prophet; (6) a man as a murderer.

There is therefore no basis for translating *anēr* "husband" rather than "father" in Matthew 1:16, and every reason from the genealogy to translate it "father." This is further authenticated from the Aramaic. *Anēr* in Matthew 1:16 is *gbra* in Aramaic, meaning "mighty man." The Aramaic word for "husband" is *bāla*, used in Matthew 1:19, "Joseph the husband [*bāla*] of Mary ...."

> Matthew 1:16 and 19:
> And Jacob begat Joseph the husband [*gbra*, mighty man] of Mary, of whom was born Jesus, who is called Christ.

> Then Joseph her husband [*bāla*], being a just *man*, and not willing to make her a publick example, was minded to put her away privily.

Biblical and Oriental customs further verify this

truth. The father who is the head of the household is the "mighty man." The son, even though a husband, is always under subjection to the father, the "mighty man," who presides over the whole household, until he, the father, dies. Then the son, who is a husband and father, becomes the head of the household, the "mighty man." The son would never be referred to as the head of the household, the "mighty man," while his father is alive.

Matthew 1:16 should read, "And Jacob begat Joseph, the father of Mary, of whom was born Jesus, who is called Christ." This translation makes the Word of God in Matthew and Luke fit perfectly, and deprives Bible critics of every argument relating to this subject of genealogy.

It is certainly acceptable and easily understood that Mary could have a father having the same name as her husband, namely, Joseph. Studying the Matthew record in detail from genealogy, the Greek word usage, the Aramaic word usage and the Biblical and Oriental customs, we conclusively discover from all four that Matthew 1:16 must be translated "Joseph the father of Mary." This then establishes the fourteen generations "from the carrying away into Babylon unto Christ."

Luke rings a striking truth in the light of the above insight.

152

Luke 3:23:

And Jesus himself began to be about thirty years of age, being (as was supposed) the son of Joseph, which was *the son** of Heli.

The purpose in setting Luke's genealogy of Joseph as the supposed father of Jesus as reckoned by Judean laws was simply to establish Jesus, whom Joseph subsequently treated as his son, with complete legal standing in the House of David.

The genealogy of Joseph, the husband of Mary, is given in Luke 3:23–38. (The ancestral line of Joseph is the legal male side.)

God

1 Adam
2. Seth
3. Enos
4. Cainan
5. Maleleel
6. Jared
7. Enoch
8. Mathusala
9. Lamech
10. Noe
11. Sem
12. Arphaxad
13. Cainan
14. Sala
15. Heber
16. Phalec
17. Ragau
18. Saruch
19. Nachor
20. Thara

*The King James Version is misleading in that it places "the son" in italics when *huios*, the son, does appear in the Stephens Greek text. This is a very grave error in the King James Version.

21. Abraham
22. Isaac
23. Jacob
24. Juda
25. Phares
26. Esrom
27. Aram
28. Aminadab
29. Naasson
30. Salmon
31. Booz
32. Obed
33. Jesse
34. David (the King)
35. Nathan
36. Mattatha
37. Menan
38. Melea
39. Eliakim
40. Jonan
41. Joseph
42. Juda
43. Simeon
44. Levi
45. Matthat
46. Jorim
47. Eliezer
48. Jose
49. Er
50. Elmodam
51. Cosam
52. Addi
53. Melchi
54. Neri
55. Salathiel
56. Zorobabel
57. Rhesa
58. Joanna
59. Juda
60. Joseph
61. Semei
62. Mattathias
63. Maath
64. Nagge
65. Esli
66. Naum
67. Amos
68. Mattathias
69. Joseph
70. Janna
71. Melchi
72. Levi
73. Matthat
74. Heli (father of Joseph)
75. Joseph (husband of Mary)

Nothing is so dynamically thrilling as tne inherent accuracy of God's wonderful, matchless Word. How truly wonderful it is to know that the Bible is the inspired Word of God and, as originally given when holy men of God recorded it as they were moved by the Holy Spirit, is absolute truth.

CHAPTER TEN

The Conception of Jesus Christ

Many people both inside and outside the church reject the divine conception of Jesus Christ. But for those of us who believe that the Word of God means what it says, we must acknowledge that Jesus was conceived in Mary by the Holy Spirit. The record of the conception and birth of Jesus Christ is clearly set forth in Matthew 1:18—25.

Now the birth of Jesus Christ was on this wise: When as his mother Mary was espoused to Joseph, before they came together, she was found with child of the Holy Ghost.

Then Joseph her husband, being a just *man*, and not willing to make her a publick example, was minded to put her away privily.

But while he thought on these things, behold, the angel of the Lord appeared unto him in a

157

dream, saying, Joseph, thou son of David, fear not to take unto thee Mary thy wife: for that which is conceived in her is of the Holy Ghost.

And she shall bring forth a son, and thou shalt call his name JESUS: for he shall save his people from their sins.

Now all this was done, that it might be fulfilled which was spoken of the Lord by the prophet, saying,

Behold, a virgin shall be with child, and shall bring forth a son, and they shall call his name Emmanuel, which being interpreted is, God with us.

Then Joseph being raised from sleep did as the angel of the Lord had bidden him, and took unto him his wife:

And knew her not till she had brought forth her firstborn son: and he called his name JESUS.

There is no question that the Bible teaches the divine conception. The question is only of the accuracy of the Bible. Is the Bible accurate when it states that Jesus was conceived by the Holy Spirit and born of Mary who was a virgin at the time of the conception?

The Bible teaches that Jesus was a sinless man. Other parts of the Bible teach that all men since Adam are born "dead in trespasses and sin." So how can we account for the sinlessness of Jesus? Jesus was born sinless — but also kept himself sinless as He aged. Hebrews gives part of the answer.

> Hebrews 2:14:
> Forasmuch then as the children are partakers of flesh and blood, he also himself likewise took part of the same....

All children are of Adam, and all partake of Adam's flesh and blood.* The word "partake" is the Greek word *koinōneō* and means to "share fully." So all of Adam's descendants *share fully* in his flesh and blood, thereby transmitting sinfulness to all Adam's children. But Jesus just "took part" of the same, the Greek word is *metechō* which means to "take only a part, not all." Jesus took some part, but not all; He did not partake, *koinōneō*, share fully. Ordinarily all children share fully in Adam's flesh and blood, but Jesus did not share fully. According to the flesh He was like Adam, but the life of the flesh in the blood of Jesus came by way of the supernatural conception by the Holy Spirit, God.

If Jesus had been conceived by sexual relationship

---

*Flesh when used as a figure of speech stands for that which is physical, while blood represents life.

between Mary and Joseph, He would have been as sinful as any other child that is born of man's seed, and would have shared fully in Adam's flesh and blood. The soul-life in the blood of Jesus came to Him not through Mary but by way of the creation of soul-life in Mary by the Holy Spirit.

Natural life, which is called "soul-life," is in the blood.* Sin is transmitted through the life in the blood which is soul-life and not through the flesh. This life which is in the blood is contributed by the sperm of the male. Soul-life is in the seed. You can understand the significance of the male's contribution when studying the conception of Jesus Christ.

The ovum has to be fertilized by the sperm to have soul-life. The mother provides the unborn, developing infant with the nutritive elements for the building of that little body within her. The placenta forming the union between mother and child is so constructed that all the nutritive elements and even antibodies pass freely from mother to child, and the waste products of the child's metabolism are passed back to the mother. There is, however, no actual interchange of blood. All the blood which is in that child is produced within the child itself.

---

*Leviticus 17:11: "For the life of the flesh *is* in the blood ...."

The Conception of Jesus Christ

How wonderfully God prepared for the birth of His Son, Jesus Christ, from the beginning. When He formed and made woman He made her so that no blood should pass directly from her to her offspring.

Adam is the head of all the races of men on earth, and Jesus had to be of the line of Adam in order to fulfill the law. God, in order to produce a sinless man and yet one who was of the line of Adam, had to provide a way whereby Jesus would have a human body derived from Adam and yet not have soul-life from Adam's sinful blood.* Jesus was sinless because He was conceived by the Holy Spirit, yet was born of Mary with a body of flesh, as all mankind.

Conception by the Holy Spirit was the only way Jesus Christ could be conceived. Mary nurtured the body of Jesus in her womb and He became the line of Adam and David according to the flesh. The Holy Spirit contributed the soul-life in the blood of Jesus by way of the sperm. In His arteries and veins there was sinless soul-life. When Judas betrayed Jesus he confessed according to Matthew 27:4, "I have betrayed the innocent blood." Sin made the original soul-life corruptible, but the soul-life of Jesus was from God.

*God created soul-life in the sperm that impregnated the ovum (egg) of Mary in the Fallopian tube. This created sperm carried only dominant characteristics and did what ordinarily any sperm would do to an egg.

161

The original sin of Adam and Eve affected the whole blood stream. Since we are partakers of the flesh and blood of Adam and Eve, our lives are contaminated to the extent that there is no hope without a Savior who had sinless soul-life; Jesus Christ purchased us with His own blood, who in Himself was deathless until He took the sin of others upon Himself and died their death. All of this because He was conceived by the Holy Spirit and born of Mary.

Mary, having conceived by the Holy Spirit, was taken by Joseph as his wife.

> Luke 1:26,27:
> And in the sixth month [of Elisabeth's pregnancy with John the Baptist] the angel Gabriel was sent from God unto a city of Galilee, named Nazareth,

> To a virgin espoused to a man whose name was Joseph, of the house of David; and the virgin's name *was* Mary.

The word "virgin" means "woman of marriageable age," while "espoused" may mean "wife" or "committed." "Espoused" means more than simply engaged; it applies to the first day of the ten days of

162

the wedding and continues to include the entire first year of marriage.

Luke 1:28—34:
And the angel came in unto her, and said, Hail, *thou that art* highly favoured, the Lord *is* with thee: blessed *art* thou among women.

And when she saw *him,* she was troubled at his saying, and cast in her mind what manner of salutation this should be.

And the angel said unto her, Fear not, Mary: for thou hast found favour with God.

And, behold, thou shalt conceive in thy womb, and bring forth a son, and shalt call his name JESUS.

He shall be great, and shall be called the Son of the Highest: and the Lord God shall give unto him the throne of his father David:

And he shall reign over the house of Jacob for ever; and of his kingdom there shall be no end.

Then said Mary unto the angel, How shall this be, seeing I know not a man?

163

Mary's "knowing not a man" means that Joseph and Mary had not yet had sexual intercourse with a resulting pregnancy. The time of the coming together was determined by the priest and elders of the city, taking into consideration the birthdates of the bride and groom. This first coming together would take place some time after the ten-day wedding ceremony on the date set by the priest and elders. Reasonably, no father and mother would negotiate a marriage unless their son or daughter would be permitted to have intercourse relatively soon after the ten days of wedding ceremonies.

> Luke 1:35:
> And the angel answered and said unto her, The Holy Ghost shall come upon thee, and the power of the Highest shall overshadow thee: therefore also that holy thing which shall be born of thee shall be called the Son of God.

The word "overshadow" means "to cover": "the power of the Highest shall cover thee." In the animal kingdom we speak of a bull covering a cow, meaning the sexual position for conception. The same meaning is evident in human beings.

> Luke 1:36–39:
> And, behold, thy cousin Elisabeth, she hath also conceived a son in her old age: and this is the

sixth month with her, who was called barren.

For with God nothing shall be impossible.

And Mary said, Behold the handmaid of the Lord; be it unto me according to thy word. And the angel departed from her.

And Mary arose in those days, and went into the hill country with haste, into a city of Juda.

Note in the last verse that there is no implication that Joseph did *not* go with Mary to the residence of Zachariah and Elisabeth.

Now, having read Luke, let us look at Matthew's account of the birth of Jesus.

Matthew 1:18—20:
Now the birth of Jesus Christ was on this wise: When as his mother Mary was espoused to Joseph, before they came together, she was found with child of the Holy Ghost.

Then Joseph her husband [it says plainly that Joseph was her husband], being a just *man* [one desiring to obey the law], and not willing to make her a publick example, was minded to put her away privily [secretly].

But while he [Joseph] thought on these things, behold, the angel of the Lord appeared unto him in a dream, saying, Joseph, thou son of David, fear not to take unto thee Mary thy wife: for that which is conceived in her is of [by] the Holy Ghost [Spirit].

In the latter part of verse 20, the angel said to Joseph, "Fear not to take unto thee Mary thy wife." "To take unto thee" means to draw close or to be intimate in sexual relations. "Take unto thee" literally means "to take her as a wife," not just to take her and watch over her until the baby is born. Mary is already the wife of Joseph so the instruction to "take unto him" would mean something more; it means intercourse. If the words in this verse had said, "Take unto thee, Mary, to be thy wife," it would be different. But it says, "Take unto thee thy wife"; Mary was already his wife.

Matthew does not specifically state how Joseph knew that Mary was pregnant. But if God could relate the news to Mary, He could certainly tell her husband, Joseph.

Joseph was explicitly told not to fear to have intercourse with his wife and also not to worry if no tokens of virginity* were present because Mary was pregnant by the Holy Spirit and not by another man.

Matthew 1:21–24:
And she shall bring forth a son, and thou shalt call his name JESUS: for he shall save his people from their sins.

Now all this was done, that it might be fulfilled which was spoken of the Lord by the prophet, saying,

Behold, a virgin shall be with child, and shall bring forth a son, and they shall call his name Emmanuel, which being interpreted is, God with us.

Then Joseph being raised from sleep did as the angel of the Lord had bidden him, and took unto him his wife.

Joseph now carried out exactly the angel's commands. He "took unto him" simply means he had intercourse with Mary. From this point on, Joseph

---

*Deuteronomy 22:15: "Then shall the father of the damsel, and her mother, take and bring forth *the tokens of* the damsel's virginity unto the elders of the city in the gate."
Deuteronomy 24:1: "When a man hath taken a wife, and married her, and it come to pass that she find no favour in his eyes, because he hath found some uncleanness in her: then let him write her a bill of divorcement, and give *it* in her hand, and send her out of his house."

and Mary lived in a normal marital relationship.

> Matthew 1:25:
> And [but] knew her not till she had brought
> forth her firstborn son: and he called his name
> JESUS.

Some commentaries and theologians declare that
Mary was a virgin when she brought forth her first
Son. According to verse 23, Mary was a virgin when
she became pregnant. But verse 24 records that
Joseph "took unto him his wife," according to the
angel's command. Even though Joseph took unto him
his wife, "he knew her not." "Knew her not" specifically has to do, not with sexual intercourse alone,
but with sexual intercourse producing pregnancy.
Even though Joseph had sexual relations with Mary
while she was pregnant with Jesus, Mary never conceived by Joseph until after Jesus Christ was born.*

"Then Joseph being raised from sleep did as the
angel ... had bidden him, and took unto him his
wife." This was announced by the angel to Joseph the
night that he and Mary were to "come together."

---

*It is possible for a woman to be pregnant again during the early days
of the first pregnancy. This verse contradicts this possibility even
though Joseph did have intercourse with Mary; she did not conceive by
him until after the birth of Jesus Christ. Matthew 13:55,56: "Is not
this the carpenter's son? is not his mother called Mary? and his
brethren, James, and Joses, and Simon, and Judas? And his sisters, are
they not all with us? Whence then hath this *man* all these things?"

Some of the Eastern religions teach that Thomas
Didymus was the twin brother of Jesus, that they
looked enough alike to pass for each other and that
after Jesus Christ was crucified the apostles mistook
Thomas Didymus for Jesus. The Word takes care of
this contention by saying "He [Joseph] took her
[Mary]" but "knew her not"; Joseph had sexual
intercourse with his wife, but Mary did not conceive
by their sexual relations until after Jesus Christ was
born.

> Genesis 4:1:
> And Adam knew Eve his wife; and she
> conceived, and bare Cain ....

> Verse 17:
> And Cain knew his wife; and she conceived, and
> bare Enoch ....

> Verse 25:
> And Adam knew his wife again [after the death
> of Abel, years later]; and she bare a son, and
> called his name Seth ....

If "to know" a wife is simply to have intercourse
then the preceding records are ridiculous.

> Genesis 19:5 and 8:
> And they called unto Lot, and said unto him,

> Where *are* the men which came in to thee this night? bring them out unto us, that we may know them.

> Behold now, I have two daughters which have not known man ....

Two daughters are mentioned in verse 8, and sons-in-law in verse 14.

> Genesis 19:14:
> And Lot went out, and spake unto his sons in law, which married his daughters ....

But verse 8 says that these two daughters "had not known man." Surely they had had intercourse, but they had not conceived.

"To know" is again demonstrated in Genesis 24.

> Genesis 24:16:
> And the damsel *was* very fair to look upon, a virgin, neither had any man known her: and she went down to the well, and filled her pitcher, and came up.

This usage of "virgin" and "known" emphasizes the damsel's purity. The word "know" again refers to not having had a child.

170

In Genesis 38 we note the record of Judah who thought the woman which he went in unto was a harlot, but discovered her to be his own daughter-in-law.

Genesis 38:18 and 26:
And he said, What pledge [plight] shall I give thee? And she said, Thy signet, and thy bracelets, and thy staff that *is* in thine hand. And he gave *it* her, and came in unto her, and she conceived by him.

And Judah acknowledged *them,* and said, She hath been more righteous than I; because that I gave her not to Shelah my son. And he [Judah] knew her again no more.

To "come in unto" does not mean the same as "knowing" her. Judah did not "go in to her" for the purpose of knowing her, of having her conceive, but it turned out that way in this incident. The Word states, "He knew her again no more," meaning that Judah never had another child by this woman.

Genesis 39:14:
That she called unto the men of her house, and spake unto them, saying, See, he hath brought in an Hebrew unto us to mock us; he came in unto me to lie with me, and I cried with a loud voice.

171

"To lie with me" infers intercourse, with or without pregnancy.

Another account of "to know" is given in Numbers 31.

> Numbers 31:17,18:
> Now therefore kill every male among the little ones, and kill every woman that hath known man [has conceived] by lying with him.
>
> But all the women children, that have not known [that have not conceived] a man by lying with him, keep alive for yourselves.

The instruction "to kill every woman that hath known man" means that at that time they were pregnant or had previously had children. It implies that you could lie with man without "knowing him." They had to be able to discriminate which women had or had not "known man."

Judges again discriminates between "intercourse" and "intercourse which produces a child."

> Judges 21:12:
> And they found among the inhabitants of Jabesh-gilead four hundred young virgins, that had known no man by lying with any male: and

they brought them unto the camp to Shiloh, which *is* in the land of Canaan.

"Four hundred young virgins, that had not known man" does not mean they had not had intercourse, but that they had not had intercourse which resulted in pregnancy. This is the third time we have come across the words "had known no man by lying with any male" or words to that effect. Either these are redundant statements or they definitely fortify the truth that "know" or "to know" means "intercourse to the end of conception."

I Samuel 1:19,20:
And they rose up in the morning early, and worshipped before the Lord, and returned, and came to their house to Ramah: and Elkanah knew Hannah his wife; and the Lord remembered her.

Wherefore it came to pass, when the time was come about after Hannah had conceived, that she bare a son, and called his name Samuel, *saying,* Because I have asked him of the Lord.

The implication is clear and plain that when "Elkanah knew Hannah his wife," she conceived.

In Matthew 1:20 the angel said to Joseph, "Fear

173

not to take unto thee Mary thy wife." In verse 25 he "knew her not till she had brought forth her first born son"; Mary had intercourse with Joseph but did not conceive by Joseph until after the birth of Jesus.* Joseph did not "know" his wife until she had been delivered of Jesus, who was conceived in Mary by the Holy Spirit.

God cannot be born but His Son our Lord and Savior Jesus Christ was conceived in Mary by God's creation of life in Mary. Thus the conception of Jesus Christ is by supernatural laws and the birth by natural law with one complementing the other and neither contrary one to the other.

---

*A few important Scripture passages pertinent to this study: Genesis 9:4; Leviticus 17:11,14; Acts 17:24-26; 20:28; Hebrews 9:22; Romans 3:25; 5:9; I Peter 1:19; I John 1:7; Revelation 1:5; 5:9; 7:14; 12:11.

174

CHAPTER ELEVEN

The Lord's Brethren

Before beginning a study of the Word of God regarding the Lord's brethren, let us first look at the historical background which made an issue of who was the Lord's family.

This question is far from new; in fact, it had become a flaming issue by 300 A.D. when Christianity west of the Euphrates River divided into two camps over the issue. The one camp was in Antioch in the country now called Turkey where Aramaic was the language spoken. The other school had its home base in Alexandria, Egypt, where Greek was the scholar's language.

The leader in the Greek school was Cyril, Bishop of Alexandria. Born into a non-Christian family, he became a Christian later in his life. In his early non-Christian days, he believed in Isis, Osiris, Horus and other such Egyptian gods. Undoubtedly this early learning influenced his thinking when he became a

175

Christian. As Bishop of Alexandria, he proposed a new doctrine, namely, that Mary was the mother of God. This idea appealed to the newly-converted Christians because their former gods had mothers, fathers, sisters and some of them had wives and even concubines. Thus the doctrine of Mary's being the mother of God fit in comfortably with their previously-held beliefs.

Heading the Antioch camp was Nestorius, a graduate of the school at Antioch and chaplain to the emperor in Constantinople. Nestorius, along with Christendom east of the River Euphrates, believed that Mary was the mother of Jesus our Lord but definitely not the mother of God. Nestorius considered Cyril's doctrine of Mary's being the mother of God a dangerous heresy.

Thus the divergent doctrines on Mary not only stirred religious controversy in the Roman Empire, but also caused a struggle over power to determine which city — Constantinople or Alexandria — was the most prominent and influential in matters of church doctrine. The Alexandrian Bishop pointed out that none of the original twelve apostles had ever gone to Constantinople or to Alexandria. But since Philip had come to Alexandria, Alexandria should be considered the more enlightened in matters dealing with doctrinal interpretation.

176

Because of this controversy a general council of all bishops was called to meet in Ephesus in 431 A.D. The Western bishops came by ships from Greece, Rome, Spain and Alexandria. The Eastern bishops, however, had to come by time-consuming land routes and so they arrived late for the meeting. Thus, before the Nestorian group of bishops arrived, the other bishops of the West had met and condemned the position of Nestorius.

Important to note in studying the history of Christianity is that this controversy affected only Western Christianity — the Roman Empire. Eastern Christianity — the Persian Empire — was unaffected by this doctrinal schism. The Christians in Persia and in Asia Minor, including Antioch and Jerusalem, continued to believe with Nestorius that Mary was the mother of the Lord Jesus but not the mother of God. The eastern part of the Roman Empire held to the same belief as Nestorius. Then Justinian the emperor issued an ultimatum stating that any Christian who did not accept Mary as the mother of God should be killed. The result of this decree was that thousands of Christians were killed. Other thousands escaped to Iran where the Persian government gave them sanctuary.

Even to this day, this Nestorian-Cyrian controversy has not been settled. The position of Cyril, the Alexandrian bishop, has been carried into the Western world by the Roman Catholic Church. Among the pagan gods and the non-Christian experience that infused Rome, the doctrinal teaching of Mary's being the mother of God found fertile ground.

Who were the Lord's brethren would never have been questioned in the Occident had it not been for the corruption which crept into Christian churches when Mary was elevated from the Biblical position of "handmaid of the Lord" as spoken of in Luke 1:38, to the exalted, non-biblical station of *theotokos,* "mother of God."

Many of the traditions of the Roman Church have their roots in Egyptian and Babylonian mythology. The Egyptian pagan deity Isis had a divine son known as Horus. The carry-over in the Roman Church from this story is that since Isis was still a virgin after Horus was born, so Mary was also a virgin after Jesus was born. Furthermore, the Roman Catholic Church teaches that Mary had no children other than Jesus our Lord and that His brothers and sisters were the children of Joseph by a former wife or that they were the Lord's cousins — children of Mary the wife of Cleophas.

The idea that Joseph was an old man or married previously before he was married to Mary has not one

178

iota of substantiation in the Scriptures. Had Joseph had older sons by a former marriage, then the Lord Jesus' legal rights to the throne of David would have been invalidated.

A study of the word "brother" as found in the Bible shows it is used in the following ways only:

1. As children of the same parent or parents.

2. As descendants of the same common stock. (Abraham as forefather: Acts 7:23,25.)

3. As fellow men. (Matthew 7:3–5; 18:15.)

4. As spiritual children. (Acts 9:17; Romans 8:29; Hebrews 2:11.)

In the Biblical passages where "the Lord's brethren" is found, only the usage as children of the same parent or parents can be applied.

Matthew 12:46:
While he yet talked to the people, behold, *his* mother and his brethren stood without, desiring to speak with him.

Verse 47:
Then one said unto him, Behold, thy mother

179

and thy brethren stand without, desiring to
speak with thee.

Matthew 13:55:
Is not this the carpenter's son? is not his mother
called Mary? and his brethren, James, and Joses,
and Simon, and Judas?

Mark 3:31:
There came then his brethren and his mother,
and, standing without, sent unto him, calling
him.

Luke 8:19:
Then came to him *his* mother and his brethren,
and could not come at him for the press.

John 7:3:
His brethren therefore said unto him, Depart
hence, and go into Judaea, that thy disciples also
may see the works that thou doest.

Verse 5:
For neither did his brethren believe in him.

Verse 10:
But when his brethren were gone up, then went
he also up unto the feast, not openly, but as it
were in secret.

180

Acts 1:14:
These all continued with one accord in prayer
and supplication, with the women, and Mary the
mother of Jesus, and with his brethren.

I Corinthians 9:5:
Have we not power to lead about a sister, a wife,
as well as other apostles, and *as* the brethren of
the Lord, and Cephas?

Galatians 1:19:
But other of the apostles saw I none, save James
the Lord's brother.

Had the brothers and sisters in these verses been
cousins only, as the Roman Catholic Prelate Jerome
theorized, the Greek word used would have been
sungenēs, which is translated "kinsman" or
"kinsfolk" or "kin" with the exception of Luke 1:36
and 58. In these two verses *sungenēs* is translated
"cousin," which cases relate not to Jesus but to
Elisabeth.

Mark 6:4:
But Jesus said unto them, A prophet is not
without honour, but in his own country, and
among his own kin, and in his own house.

Luke 1:36:
And, behold, thy cousin Elisabeth, she hath also conceived a son in her old age: and this is the sixth month with her, who was called barren.

Luke 1:58:
And her neighbours and her cousins heard how the Lord had shewed great mercy upon her; and they rejoiced with her.

Luke 2:44:
But they, supposing him to have been in the company, went a day's journey; and they sought him among *their* kinsfolk and acquaintance.

Luke 14:12:
Then said he also to him that bade him, When thou makest a dinner or a supper, call not thy friends, nor thy brethren, neither thy kinsmen, nor *thy* rich neighbours; lest they also bid thee again, and a recompence be made thee.

Luke 21:16:
And ye shall be betrayed both by parents, and brethren, and kinsfolks, and friends; and *some* of you shall they cause to be put to death.

John 18:26:
One of the servants of the high priest, being *his*

kinsman whose ear Peter cut off, saith, Did not I see thee in the garden with him?

Acts 10:24:
And the morrow after they entered into Caesarea. And Cornelius waited for them, and had called together his kinsmen and near friends.

Romans 9:3:
For I could wish that myself were accursed from Christ for my brethren, my kinsmen according to the flesh.

Romans 16:7:
Salute Andronicus and Junia, my kinsmen, and my fellowprisoners, who are of note among the apostles, who also were in Christ before me.

Verse 11:
Salute Herodion my kinsman. Greet them that be of the *household* of Narcissus, which are in the Lord.

Verse 21:
Timotheus my workfellow, and Lucius, and Jason, and Sosipater, my kinsmen, salute you.

According to Matthew 13:55 our Lord Jesus Christ had four brothers or half-brothers as we would call them. James, Joses, Simon and Judas had the same mother but a different father. (Jesus Christ was the Son of God, by way of Mary, but conceived by the Holy Spirit.) Furthermore, Jesus had *at least* three sisters, according to Matthew 13:56: "His sisters, are they not all with us?" Had there been just two sisters the word *both* would have been used instead of *all.*

The Lord Jesus was Mary's *firstborn,** not her *only born.*† The word "firstborn" automatically implies "second born" or "later born" children. Jesus was, as the Scriptures clearly state, the "firstborn" of Mary but the "only begotten of the Father."

When all the Biblical data is in hand, we are left with a plain answer regarding the Lord's brethren. We know that He had four brothers — James, Joses, Simon and Judas — and that He had at least three sisters, whose names are not given. Beyond this, nothing is known except for idle speculation or theorizing — which is not good enough when dealing with Biblical matters.

*The meaning of the word "firstborn," which in the Greek is *prōtotokos,* can be easily ascertained from looking at its only usages in Matthew 1:25; Luke 2:7; Romans 8:29; Colossians 1:15,18; Hebrews 1:6; 11:28; 12:23 and Revelation 1:5.

†Had Jesus Christ been Mary's *only* son, the Greek word would be *monogenēs* which is used in Luke 7:12; 8:42; 9:38; John 1:14,18; 3:16,18; Hebrews 11:17; I John 4:9.

184

Part IV

Jesus Christ the End of the Law

Part IV

Jesus Christ the End of the Law

The purpose of the second Adam, Jesus Christ, was to fulfill the Old Testament law and to provide a way by which mankind could be redeemed from sin and its consequences. In order to accomplish this, sinless blood had to be spilled.

The events surrounding this most important occasion of the shedding of blood are carefully recorded in each Gospel. But accurate studies are rarities. Much erroneous teaching envelopes the events leading up to and including the death and burial of Jesus. The following research demands that the reader eliminate ungrounded ideas he has had and artist's interpretations which he has seen and look only at the Word of God itself. Only The Word can truly illuminate our hearts and minds.

"The Day Jesus Christ Died" examines the timing of Jesus' death. No one can possibly calculate three days and three nights from Good Friday afternoon to

185

Easter Sunday morning. "Did Jesus Keep the Passover?" looks at the relationship of Jesus' Last Supper to the Hebrew Passover in the year Jesus Christ was sacrificed. "Simon of Cyrene and the Cross Christ Bore" studies the events between Pilate's Judgment Hall and Jesus' crucifixion on Calvary and their significance. "The Four Crucified With Jesus" fits the four Gospel records together and clearly shows that four men, not two, were crucified with Jesus.

All the active participants and the timing are studied in "The Burial of Jesus." And finally a truly edifying truth is uncovered in Jesus' words before He died. *Eli, Eli, lmana sabachthani* was His "Cry of Triumph."

CHAPTER TWELVE

The Day Jesus Christ Died

For people to say that Jesus died on Good Friday and arose on Easter Sunday morning is not only doing great damage to the integrity of God's Word, but is also causing many people to question the simple logic of Bible believers who propound such teaching. Jesus Christ explicitly declared in Matthew that He would be in the grave three days and three nights.

> Matthew 12:40:
> For as Jonas was three days and three nights in the whale's belly; so shall the Son of man be three days and three nights in the heart of the earth.

Matthew 12:40 in twice specifying three days and three nights distinctly denotes three periods of twenty-four hours each. How can a person calculate three days and three nights from Good Friday 3:00 P.M. until Easter Sunday Morning? The Bible declares that Jesus Christ was already risen by Easter Sunday morning which would be the third day; but even so, where is the third night? This teaching does not fit. What are we going to do? We have to go to the Word of God to find the day, the hour and the details involved in Jesus' crucifixion, burial and resurrection in order to have the Word of God rightly divided. When the Word of God fits, there are no contradictions, no errors.

I Corinthians 5:7 says, "... Christ our passover is sacrificed for us." Jesus Christ in fulfilling the law had to carry out exactly the demands thereof. One important part of the law was the observance of the Passover which was first established as Moses and Aaron prepared to lead the children of Israel out of Egypt.

> Exodus 12:1—6:
> And the Lord spake unto Moses and Aaron in the land of Egypt, saying,
>
> This month *shall be* unto you the beginning of months: it *shall be* the first month [Abib or Nisan] of the year to you.*

*Exodus 13:4: "This day came ye out in the month Abib." The name of the month Abib was later, after the Babylonian captivity, changed to the month Nisan by the Babylonians. Esther 3:7, which was written after the Babylonians captivity, says, "In the first month, that is, the month of Nisan ...."

Speak ye unto all the congregation of Israel, saying, In the tenth *day* of this month they shall take to them every man a lamb, according to the house of *their* fathers, a lamb for an house:

And if the household be too little for the lamb, let him and his neighbour next unto his house take *it* according to the number of the souls; every man according to his eating shall make your count for the lamb.

Your lamb shall be without blemish, a male of the first year: ye shall take *it* out from the sheep, or from the goats:

And ye shall keep it up until the fourteenth day of the same month: and the whole assembly of the congregation of Israel shall kill it in the evening.

The tenth to the fourteenth of the first month (Abib or Nisan) are days to prepare for the high day of Passover. The first day of the Passover was always on the fifteenth of Nisan.

Leviticus 23:5:
In the fourteenth *day* of the first month at even [evening] *is* the Lord's passover.

189

The fourteenth day at even began the fifteenth of Nisan as the Jewish day begins at sunset, the even. The fourteenth was the day before the Passover, the Feast of Unleavened Bread, the day of preparation. On the fifteenth of Nisan the Passover Feast officially began.

> Leviticus 23:6,7:
> And on the fifteenth day of the same month *is* the feast of unleavened bread [which is Passover] unto the Lord: seven days ye must eat unleavened bread.
>
> In the first day ye shall have an holy convocation ....

The first day of the Feast of Unleavened Bread, the fifteenth, would always be a holy convocation, a Sabbath day, a high day.

If the first day of the Feast of Unleavened Bread came on a Tuesday, that Tuesday would be a Sabbath day. If the first day of the Feast came on a weekly Sabbath, on a Saturday, then it still was a high day and it would have pre-eminence over the weekly Sabbath. This pre-eminence is similar to our holidays. For example, if Christmas happens to come on a Tuesday, it is a holiday; but if Christmas comes on a Sunday, the special day of Christmas takes priority over the weekly Sunday. This point has bearing upon the death and resurrection of our Lord Jesus Christ.

The greatest point of confusion comes by not differentiating between the Sabbath which was the first day of the Feast of Unleavened Bread and the weekly Sabbath. The day before the weekly Sabbath was Friday so the teaching has therefore been that Jesus died on Friday. But the day after Jesus' death does not refer to the weekly Sabbath, as explicitly stated in John.

> John 19:31:
> The Jews therefore, because it was the preparation [the day before the fifteenth of Nisan], that the bodies should not remain upon the cross on the sabbath day, (for that sabbath day was an high day,) besought Pilate that their legs might be broken, and *that* they might be taken away.

The fact that Jesus was crucified before a special Sabbath is emphasized in the King James by putting the notation in parentheses: "... (for that sabbath day was an high day,) ...." Jesus was crucified the day before a special day, the high day, which was the first

191

day of the Feast of Unleavened Bread, the Passover, and not on the day before the regular weekly Sabbath.

The Gospels document the specific time of day that Jesus Christ died on the fourteenth of Nisan.

Matthew 27:45,46,50:
Now from the sixth hour there was darkness over all the land unto the ninth hour.

And about the ninth hour Jesus cried with a loud voice ....

Jesus, when he had cried again with a loud voice, yielded up the ghost.

Mark 15:33,34,37:
And when the sixth hour was come, there was darkness over the whole land until the ninth hour.

And at the ninth hour Jesus cried with a loud voice ....

And Jesus cried with a loud voice, and gave up the ghost.

Luke 23:44—46:
And it was about the sixth hour, and there was a
darkness over all the earth until the ninth hour.

And the sun was darkened, and the veil of the
temple was rent in the midst.

And when Jesus had cried with a loud voice, he
said, Father, into thy hands I commend my
spirit: and having said thus, he gave up the
ghost.

After Pilate released Jesus to the Jews, John
19:15—30 records Jesus' being led away to Golgotha,
His crucifixion, the title being nailed above Jesus'
head, His clothes being parted, the attention given to
His mother and His receiving the vinegar. Then verse
30 repeats the account of Jesus' death.

John 19:30,31:
When Jesus therefore had received the vinegar,
he said, It is finished: and he bowed his head,
and gave up the ghost.

The Jews therefore, because it was the preparation, that the bodies should not remain upon the
cross on the sabbath day, (for that sabbath day
was an high day,) ....

The day and time of the crucifixion and burial are clearly on the fourteenth of the first month between three and six o'clock in the afternoon. All four Gospels also readily concur on the time of the resurrection of Jesus Christ.

Three o'clock was the time of death. To fulfill the Passover rite, Jesus, our sacrificial lamb, had to be buried sometime between 3 P.M. and sunset, for after sunset began the high day and thereon no one could do manual labor.

Leviticus 23:7:
In the first day ye shall have an holy convocation: ye shall do no servile work therein.

Joseph of Arimathea had to work quickly after Jesus' death to get permission from Pilate, to remove Jesus' body and to place it in his newly-hewn tomb.

John 19:41,42:
Now in the place where he was crucified there was a garden; and in the garden a new sepulchre, wherein was never man yet laid.

There laid they Jesus therefore because of the Jews' preparation *day;* for the sepulchre was nigh at hand.

These four records pinpoint the day of Jesus' crucifixion and burial as being the day before the Passover,
the fourteenth of Nisan, and the time of Jesus' death
as being the ninth hour, which by our reckoning of
time is three o'clock in the afternoon.

Matthew 28:1:
In the end of the sabbath [this is the weekly
sabbath], as it began to dawn toward the first
day of the week [our Sunday], came Mary Magdalene and the other Mary to see the sepulchre.

This is early Sunday morning. In verse 6 of
Matthew 28 the report was, "He is not here: for he is
risen ...." This verse does not say that He arose on
what is called Easter Sunday morning. It says that by
the time the women got to the tomb, the angel
reported that Jesus was not there for He had already
risen.

Mark 16:1 and 6:
And when the sabbath was past, Mary
Magdalene, and Mary the *mother* of James, and
Salome, had bought sweet spices, that they
might come and anoint him.

And he [the angel] saith unto them, Be not
affrighted: Ye seek Jesus of Nazareth, which was

crucified: he is risen; he is not here: behold the place where they laid him.

Mark does not say that Jesus had just arisen. The declaration of the angel again was, "He is already up."

Again in Luke 24:6 the angel declared to those at the sepulchre on Sunday morning, "He is not here, but is risen ...." Once more, The Word simply declares that He was already up. It does not tell in Matthew, Mark nor Luke exactly when He got up; but it does tell that by the time the women came, which was very early, Christ had already risen. John 20:1 records that when Mary Magdalene arrived at the sepulchre in the dark of the early morning of the "first *day* of the week," the tomb was empty. Not one of the Gospels — Matthew, Mark, Luke nor John — states that Christ arose on Easter Sunday morning. That is tradition, not The Word.

Matthew 12:40 states that Jesus was not simply to be dead three days and three nights; He was to be buried three days and three nights. A legal standard is involved in the "three days and three nights in the heart of the earth." In Biblical times no one could be officially pronounced dead until he had been interred for seventy-two hours, three days and three nights. Why did God not raise His Son immediately after

Jesus died, since God obviously had the power? The reason lies in the legality of the event, for Jesus Christ had to fulfill the law; that is, He had to be in the grave three days and three nights and not just part of this time.

Our failure to recognize that the first day of the Passover was a high Sabbath, a holy day, a special convocation, and our failure to understand that the Jewish day began at sunset have caused most of the difficulty regarding the time of the death and resurrection of Jesus Christ.

The Bible says in John 19:31 that Jesus was crucified and buried on the day of preparation, the fourteenth day of Nisan. Matthew 27:46 tells us that Jesus died at 3:00 P.M., which is the ninth hour by Jewish reckoning. Jesus had to be buried before sunset because sunset started the next day, which was the Passover. To get three complete nights and days beginning with the late afternoon of the fourteenth of Nisan, the seventy-two hour duration would end with the late afternoon of the seventeenth of Nisan. So at whatever time He was buried between 3:00 and sunset on the fourteenth of Nisan was the hour He was raised on the seventeenth of Nisan — seventy-two hours later. Now we must count backward to calculate the days of the week.

We know that when Mary Magdalene came to the tomb early on Sunday, the first day of the week, the tomb was already empty and Christ had already risen. So Christ had to have risen sometime between 3:00 P.M. and sunset on *Saturday*, the seventeenth of Nisan. That means He would have had to have been buried between 3:00 P.M. and sunset on *Wednesday*, the fourteenth of Nisan, three days and three nights or seventy-two hours previously. Jesus Christ literally fulfilled the law; He carried out the Word of God by being buried on Wednesday afternoon and being raised seventy-two hours later on Saturday afternoon.

Jesus Christ literally fulfilled the law. While the Jews selected their spotless lamb to be used as the Passover sacrifice, Jesus Christ was "selected" and acknowledged as acceptable when He made His triumphal entry into Jerusalem. While the Passover lamb was being sacrificed in the late afternoon during the preparation, Jesus Christ was dying on Golgotha. The blood of the Passover lamb was of non-effect beginning with this occasion as Jesus was the true Passover, the complete Passover.

However, just because Jesus died on a Wednesday, I am not going to advocate that we change to Good Wednesday instead of Good Friday for Galatians 4:9 and 10 says that we are not to be observers of days or times or special hours. But I am going to adhere to

198

the accuracy of God's Word and acknowledge its truth. The pieces of the puzzle fall into place when the days of the months are rightly divided, when the hours of the days are rightly divided, and when the special days are understood. These tie together the whole record of the death and resurrection of Jesus Christ. The Word of God is always so accurate.

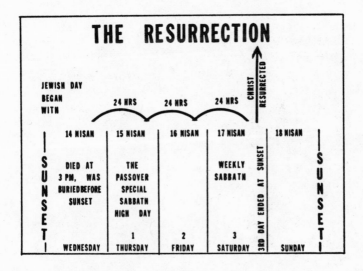

CHAPTER THIRTEEN

Did Jesus Keep the Passover?

Theology teaches that Jesus' Last Supper was also the annual Hebrew Passover meal. However, the Scriptures plainly teach that Jesus Christ died on the fourteenth of Nisan, the day before the Passover.* He could not, therefore, have eaten the Hebrew Passover meal as He was dead and buried before that time. To substantiate that the Last Supper was not the Passover, we will consider every reference to the Last Supper in its Biblical context. First though, let us set some basic information.

1. The preparation for the Passover is a preliminary part of the sacrifice, just as much as the preparation for a dinner occurs before eating the dinner.
2. The fifteenth day of Nisan was the Passover Day and the Feast of Unleavened Bread. During the days before the Passover, the people had to

*See Chapter 12, "The Day Jesus Christ Died."

specifically prepare themselves, their homes and the sacrifice and thus make ready for the Passover. This activity is spoken of in John 19:42 as the Jew's preparation.

a. The Temple, if defiled, had to be cleansed. II Chronicles 29:4, 5.

b. The homes of the people had to be cleansed. Exodus 12:15, 19.

c. The priests and Levites had to be cleansed. II Chronicles 30.

d. The individual person had to be cleansed. John 11:55; Hebrews 9:13, 14; Numbers 9:6.

3. Five days preceding the Passover, thus on the tenth of Nisan, according to Exodus 12:3–6, the sacrificial lamb was carefully selected and groomed properly until the fourteenth of Nisan. The five days beginning with the tenth of Nisan are an integral part of the preparation and sacrifice. Thus, logically the Passover began before it *officially* started in the sense that the preparations for it were begun.

Technically, the preparation had started at the time the Passover lamb was selected on the tenth of Nisan. The lamb was then killed on the fourteenth; it was eaten after sunset and during the night following its killing which was, according to Jewish reckoning of time, the fifteenth of Nisan.

4. A human author may, for impact or emphasis.

jump from one major event to the next in his story, skipping minor incidents in between. Later he may give the in-between events. So God, in His Word, set the Last Supper of the Lord Jesus Christ immediately following details of the preparation for the Passover even though these events were separated by several days.

Keeping these fundamental truths in mind, we may now proceed with the study of the Last Supper and its relation to the Hebrew Passover. We will look first at the record in the Gospel of John because it sets the time of the Last Supper most clearly.

John 13:1:

Now before the feast of the passover, when Jesus knew that his hour was come that he should depart out of this world unto the Father, having loved his own which were in the world, he loved them unto the end.

Verse 2:

And supper being ended, the devil having now put into the heart of Judas Iscariot, Simon's *son*, to betray him.

John is the only Gospel that does not record the actual initiating of the memorial of Jesus' suffering and death. However verse 1 does tell us that Jesus knew the hour of his death and that this was, according to verse 2, at the time of His Last Supper with His disciples. Later then, in verses 26 and 27 of John 13, John tells us of the disciples' feet being washed by Jesus, and Jesus' giving the sop to Judas Iscariot. The rest of chapter 13 and chapters 14—17 give the account of Jesus' teachings to His disciples. In John 18:1 we read, "When Jesus had spoken these words, he went forth with his disciples over the brook Cedron, where was a garden, into the which he entered, and his disciples."

The major incidents concerning the Last Supper which are covered in the Gospel of John are as follows:

1. The Last Supper — John 13:2.
    (Jesus knew His hour of death)

2. His betrayal foretold by Him — John 13:21.

3. The betrayer revealed (the sop given) — John 13:26. (The memorial bread and cup, omitted at this point)

4. Peter's denial foretold — John 13:38.

5. The garden where He prayed — John 18:1.

The actual memorial is not recorded. John's record

gives more emphasis to the betrayal being told and the revealing of the betrayer.

With this background now let us read Luke's account of the Last Supper.

Luke 22:1:
Now the feast of unleavened bread drew nigh, which is called the Passover.

Verse 7:
Then came the day* [time] of unleavened bread, when the passover must be killed [prepared].

The word "killed" in the King James is the Greek word *thuō*. It means "to get ready or prepare the sacrifice and later to kill it." (See Points 1, 2, 3 on pages 201, 202.)

Luke 22:13,14:
... and they made ready the passover.

And when the hour was come, he [Jesus] sat down, and the twelve apostles with him [at the Last Supper].

---

*The word "day" frequently refers to a period of time as here in Luke 22:7. The Estrangelo Aramaic word, *ioma*, is variously translated day, month, aged, after some time, etc.

"The hour" must be the Last Supper as seen by the rest of the context. This verse begins a new subject, the Last Supper.

> Luke 22:15:
> And he said unto them, With desire [great earnestness] I have desired to eat this passover [this impending feast which would take place on the 15th of Nisan] with you before I suffer.

The words "with desire I have desired" are the figure of speech *polypototon* meaning "the same root word with different inflexions or forms." Therefore this figure of speech is emphasizing the great desire Jesus had. "I have desired" are in the Greek aorist tense indicating a one-time action in the past. "At one time I *did* desire to eat this impending Passover with you." The words "I suffer" are also in the Greek aorist tense. However, being used in the infinitive mood they indicate nothing as to time, but only a one-time action. Jesus' suffering and death at this time were still future and, of course, a one-time action. Again we see the minute accuracy of God's Word.

> Luke 22:16:
> For I say unto you, I will not any more eat thereof, until it be fulfilled in the kingdom of God.

206

The reason Jesus *had* desired to eat the impending Passover with His disciples was that He knew He would "not drink of the fruit of the vine until the Kingdom of God shall come" — He would not be with them for any future Passovers. However, He now knew, at the time of the Last Supper, that He would not eat this year's Passover with them either. He, therefore, told the disciples what had been the desire of His heart as of two days before when He told them to make preparations for the Passover.* He now knew that His desire to eat the Hebrew Passover with them would not be fulfilled. Up until the Last Supper Jesus only knew that He would be crucified after two days, so He made preparation to keep the Hebrew Passover with His disciples, thinking this would be their last time to do so together. But when He spoke at the gathering now called the Last Supper, He knew that He would not partake of the Passover meal.

The major events concerning the Last Supper covered in the Gospel of Luke are as follows:

1. The Last Supper — Luke 22:14.
   (Jesus now knew His hour of death, John 13:1, 2. The telling of His betrayal is omitted here)

*Matthew 26:2, "Ye know that after two days is *the feast of* the passover, and the Son of man is betrayed to be crucified." Mark 14:1, "After two days was *the feast of* the passover, and of unleavened bread .... "

2. The memorial, bread and cup — Luke 22:17—20.

3. The betrayer revealed — Luke 22:21.

4. Peter's denial foretold — Luke 22:34.

5. The garden (place) where He prayed — Luke 22:40.

In the Gospel of Luke the order of the records of the memorial and the revealing of the betrayer are reversed. However, this record in Luke is emphasizing the instituting of the memorial rather than the betrayal, which is omitted, and the revealing of the betrayer, which is covered in one verse. The betrayer is never even named until verse forty-seven.

We will now proceed to the Gospel of Mark, the shortest of the four Gospels. The truths in this Gospel are very brief and to the point. Again the betrayer is not named until the actual betrayal took place.

Mark 14:1:
After two days was *the feast of* the passover, and of unleavened bread ....

Verse 12:
And the first day of unleavened bread, when they killed [prepared] the passover ....

"First day" refers to the first part, like we speak regarding the "first day of the Christmas Season," meaning November 25th or whatever day we start getting ready. "Killed" again means "got ready or prepared and later killed."

> Mark 14:16:
> ... they made ready [made preparation for] the passover.

> Verse 17:
> And in the evening he cometh with the twelve.

This verse begins a new subject in both time and content, namely, the Last Supper. Again it cannot be the Passover as Jesus was already dead by the time it was eaten.

> Mark 14:22:
> And as they did eat [Jesus instituted the memorial of His coming suffering and death.] ....

The major events concerning the Last Supper covered in the Gospel of Mark are as follows:

1. The Last Supper — Mark 17:17.
   (Jesus now knew the hour of His death, John 13:1, 2)

2. His betrayal foretold by Him — Mark 14:18.

3. The betrayer not actually revealed, only hinted at — Mark 14:20, 21.

4. The memorial, bread and cup — Mark 14:22–24.

5. Peter's denial foretold — Mark 14:30.

6. The garden where He prayed (Gethsemane) — Mark 14:32.

The only Gospel record left is that in Matthew. We will now add the information contained in Matthew to our preceding study.

Matthew 26:2:
Ye know that after two days is *the feast of* the passover, and the Son of man is betrayed to be crucified.

"After two days" indicates after two days have passed. Therefore, it would actually be in the third day, the fourteenth of Nisan. (See Point 3 on page 202.)

Matthew 26:17:
Now the first *day* of the *feast of* unleavened bread the disciples came to Jesus, saying unto him, Where wilt thou that we prepare for thee to eat the passover?

"Day" and "feast of" are italicized in the Authorized Version, which means these words were not in the Greek text used for the translation, but were supplied by the translators. The text says exactly what it means without the italicized words. "The first of the unleavened bread" according to Exodus 12:3 is the first part of the preparation, that part of getting the lamb ready for the Feast of Unleavened Bread. This started with the selection of the sacrificial lamb on the tenth of Nisan. Since in the year of Jesus' death the tenth of Nisan came on a *weekly* Sabbath, the Jews could not have begun to prepare on that day; they began the next day, Sunday.*

At this time on the eleventh of Nisan, Jesus knew the day (verse two) but not the hour of His death, yet He knew He was to die. Since He always fulfilled the law, and since He did not know the hour of His death, He made arrangements for keeping the Passover.

Matthew 26:18,19:
And he [Jesus] said, Go into the city to such a man, and say unto him, The Master saith, My time is at hand; I will keep the passover at thy house with my disciples.

*See chapter 12, "The Day Jesus Christ Died."

And the disciples did as Jesus had appointed them; and they made ready the passover. [They prepared for the Passover as Jesus had instructed them.]

"I will" in verse 18 is the same as "I have desired" in Luke. Remember, Jesus at this time did not know the hour of His death, and He desired to keep the Hebrew Passover with His disciples for the last time.

Matthew 26:20:
Now when the even was come, he sat down with the twelve.

"The even" again is at the time of the Last Supper as we have seen from all the other Gospels. The disciples had made ready for them to eat the Passover, but at the time of the Last Supper Jesus first knew that He would not live to eat the Hebrew Passover with them.

The major events concerning the Last Supper covered in the Gospel of Matthew are as follows:

1. The Last Supper — Matthew 26:20
   (Jesus now knew the hour of His death, John 13:1, 2)

2. His betrayal foretold by Him — Matthew 26:21.

3. The betrayer revealed — Matthew 26:23.

4. The memorial, bread and cup — Matthew 26:26–28.

5. Peter's denial foretold — Matthew 26:34.

6. The garden where He prayed (Gethsemane) — Matthew 26:36.

All four Gospels pointedly show that Jesus ate the Last Supper, but He did not eat the Passover. According to I Corinthians the Passover lamb that year was once and for all Jesus Christ who was the Lamb of God.

> I Corinthians 5:7:
> Purge out therefore the old leaven, that ye may be a new lump, as ye are unleavened. For even Christ our passover is sacrificed for us.

Jesus Christ gave His life on the same day at the *simultaneous time* that the Hebrew Passover lamb was slain. Jesus was the authentic Passover lamb, although the Judeans did not know it. Jesus ate the Last Supper with the twelve disciples, *not* the Hebrew Passover. The Hebrew Passover lamb was to be eaten while standing (Exodus 12:11), but Jesus sat down with the twelve as they ate (Matthew 26:20).

213

For the sacrificial Passover lamb that year, God supplied Jesus Christ, who was forever *the Passover* for all who will be saved. Not as a yearly sacrifice or as a "mass," but as having entered in once and for all. During the Last Supper, Jesus Christ instituted what today we call the Lord's Supper. Jesus Christ instituted the bread and cup as a memorial of His sacrifice that night, to be kept by His brethren until He comes again.

Matthew 26:26–28:
And as they were eating, Jesus took bread, and blessed *it*, and brake *it*, and gave *it* to the disciples, and said, Take, eat; this is my body.

And he took the cup, and gave thanks, and gave *it* to them, saying, Drink ye all of it;

For this is my blood of the new testament, which is shed for many for the remission of sins.

Mark 14:22–24:
And as they did eat, Jesus took bread, and blessed, and brake *it*, and gave to them, and said, Take, eat: this is my body.

And he took the cup, and when he had given thanks, he gave *it* to them: and they all drank of it.

214

And he said unto them, This is my blood of the new testament, which is shed for many.

Luke 22:15-20:
And he said unto them, With desire I have desired to eat this passover with you before I suffer:

For I say unto you, I will not any more eat thereof, until it be fulfilled in the kingdom of God.

And he took the cup, and gave thanks, and said, Take this, and divide *it* among yourselves:

For I say unto you, I will not drink of the fruit of the vine, until the kingdom of God shall come.

And he took bread, and gave thanks, and brake *it,* and gave unto them, saying, This is my body which is given for you: this do in remembrance of me.

Likewise also the cup after supper, saying, This cup *is* the new testament in my blood, which is shed for you.

"This is my body" is a figure of speech called a

metaphor. A *metaphor* centers on the verb "is" and *can never* be read, "is changed into." The word "represents" can replace the verb "is" in the metaphor because the verb is only figurative, not literal, and its grammatical meaning is "represents."*

The Last Supper was the establishing and ratifying of the new covenant as recorded in Jeremiah.

> Jeremiah 31:31-34:
> Behold, the days come, saith the Lord, that I will make a new covenant with the house of Israel, and with the house of Judah:
>
> Not according to the covenant that I made with their fathers in the day *that* I took them by the hand to bring them out of the land of Egypt; which my covenant they brake, although I was an husband unto them, saith the Lord:
>
> But this *shall be* the covenant that I will make with the house of Israel; After those days, saith

---

*Matthew 13:38,39: "The field is the world; the good seed are the children of the kingdom; but the tares are the children of the wicked *one;* The enemy that sowed them is the devil; the harvest is the end of the world; and the reapers are the angels."

I Corinthians 11:25: "After the same manner also *he took* the cup, when he had supped, saying, This cup is the new testament in my blood: this do ye, as oft as ye drink *it,* in remembrance of me."

I Corinthians 10:16: "The cup of blessing which we bless, is it not the communion of the blood of Christ? The bread which we break, is it not the communion of the body of Christ?"

the Lord, I will put my law in their inward parts, and write it in their hearts; and will be their God, and they shall be my people.

And they shall teach no more every man his neighbour, and every man his brother, saying, Know the Lord: for they shall all know me, from the least of them unto the greatest of them, saith the Lord: for I will forgive their iniquity, and I will remember their sin no more.

During this supper Jesus instituted the bread and cup* as a memorial, or as a substitute for the Hebrew Pascal Lamb for He was to be "cut off." The "bread" represented His body and the "cup" His atoning and covenant blood. By His "body" we have our healing and by His "blood" we have remission and forgiveness of sins.†

So we see from both this study and the previous chapter, "The Day Jesus Christ Died," that Jesus did *not* keep the Passover at all the year He gave His life, for *He* was the Passover Lamb that year and from thenceforth. He did eat a "Last Supper" with His

---

*A word more about "the cup." Paul calls it "the cup of blessing" (I Corinthians 10:16). This was the joyous climax of the occasion closing with the singing of a hymn. (Mark 14:26) This hymn may have been Psalms 115-118.

†I Peter 2:24: "Who his own self bare our sins in his own body on the tree, that we, being dead to sins, should live unto righteousness: by whose stripes ye were healed."

disciples which would have been before the four-teenth of Nisan, for the Passover Lamb (Jesus) was killed at three o'clock on the fourteenth of Nisan. How free from error and contradiction is The Word when we read what is written.

CHAPTER FOURTEEN

Simon of Cyrene
and the Cross Christ Bore

Most of us are acquainted with the generally accepted teaching that Jesus appeared before Pilate, who later had Jesus scourged. After the scourging, the soldiers put the heavy cross on Him to carry to Calvary. Then, as the soldiers and Jesus approached Calvary, Jesus broke down under the burden of the cross so the soldiers pulled Simon of Cyrene out of the crowd and ordered him to carry the cross. Simon then carried the cross all the way to Calvary where the soldiers crucified Jesus. This teaching makes for a beautiful word-picture, colorful stained glass windows in churches and an absorbing story, *but* it is not true.

To discover the accuracy of The Word regarding the cross Christ bore, let us consider separately each record in the Gospels, beginning with the Gospel of Matthew. We'll pick up the account as Jesus stood in Pilate's judgment hall, the Praetorium.

Jesus Christ the End of the Law

Matthew 27:27–32:

Then the soldiers of the governor took Jesus into the common hall, and gathered unto him the whole band *of soldiers.*

And they stripped him, and put on him a scarlet robe.

And when they had platted a crown of thorns, they put *it* upon his head, and a reed in his right hand: and they bowed the knee before him, and mocked him, saying, Hail, King of the Jews!

And they spit upon him, and took the reed, and smote him on the head.

And after they had mocked him, they took the robe off from him, and put his own raiment on him, and led him away to crucify *him.*

And as they came out [of the hall], they found a man of Cyrene, Simon by name: him they compelled to bear his cross.

As the group emerged from the judgment hall, they found a man at the entrance, and "him they compelled to bear his cross." There is nothing in the Gospel of Matthew teaching that Christ even touched the wooden cross.

220

Simon of Cyrene and the Cross Christ Bore

Simon of Cyrene was compelled to bear the cross all the way to Calvary.

Mark 15:16–21:
And the soldiers led him [Jesus] away into the hall, called Praetorium; and they call together the whole band.

And they clothed him with purple, and platted a crown of thorns, and put it about his *head*,

And began to salute him, Hail, King of the Jews!

And they smote him on the head with a reed, and did spit upon him, and bowing *their* knees worshipped him.

And when they had mocked him, they took off the purple from him, and put his own clothes on him, and led him out to crucify him.

And they compel one Simon a Cyrenian, who passed by ... to bear his cross.

Passed by where? Passed by the hall. There is no record in the Gospel of Mark that even hints that Jesus touched a piece of wood, a tree or anything like it. The Word is explicit, plain and simple.

Luke 23:20—26:
Pilate therefore, willing to release Jesus, spake again to them.

But they cried, saying, Crucify *him,* crucify him.

And he said unto them the third time, Why, what evil hath he done? I have found no cause of death in him: I will therefore chastise him, and let *him* go.

And they were instant with loud voices, requiring that he might be crucified. And the voices of them and of the chief priests prevailed.

And Pilate gave sentence that it should be as they required.

And he released unto them him that for sedition and murder was cast into prison, whom they had desired; but he delivered Jesus to their will.

And as they led him away, [note carefully] they laid hold upon one Simon, a Cyrenian, coming out of the country, and on him they laid the cross, that he might bear *it* after Jesus.

As they led Jesus away, right there outside the hall's doorway was Simon, a Cyrenian, coming out of

222

the country from the region beyond the gates. On him, not on Jesus, was laid the cross. Note the word "after." Some say the word "after" means he carried it after Jesus had carried it. No, Jesus went ahead and Simon followed behind, *after,* him.

John 19:13–17:
When Pilate therefore heard that saying, he brought Jesus forth, and sat down in the judgment seat in a place that is called the Pavement, but in the Hebrew, Gabbatha.

And it was the preparation of the passover, and about the sixth hour [twelve midnight] : and he saith unto the Jews, Behold your King!

But they cried out, Away with *him,* away with *him,* crucify him. Pilate saith unto them, Shall I crucify your King? The chief priests answered, We have no king but Caesar.

Then delivered he him therefore unto them to be crucified. And they took Jesus, and led *him* away.

And he bearing his cross went forth into a place called *the place* of the skull, which is called in the Hebrew Golgotha.

"And he [Jesus], bearing his cross ..." is the phrase from which has been inferred that Jesus bore the wooden cross. This does not agree with the clear record in the other three Gospels. The first three Gospels state very plainly that Simon bore the cross from the door of the judgment hall. But, the Gospel of John states, "And he, bearing his cross went forth into a place called *the place* of a skull." "His cross" was not wooden, but spiritual.

The cross Jesus bore was composed of our sins and our transgressions. If it had been a wooden cross, what good would that have accomplished? He did not bear a piece of wood nor a tree. He bore our sins! Note that Colossians and Isaiah tell in part, at least, about the kind of cross Jesus bore.

> Colossians 2:14:
> Blotting out the handwriting of ordinances that was against us, which was contrary to us, and took it out of the way, nailing it to his [His] cross.

> Isaiah 53:6:
> All we like sheep have gone astray; we have turned every one to his own way; and the Lord hath laid on him the iniquity of us all.

He took all the faults that were against us – the

transgressions, the sins, the bondage, the sickness and the pain — and made them a part of His cross.

The Orientalism in verse 14 of Colossians 2 must be understood in the light of Isaiah 40:2, "... that her iniquity is pardoned: for she hath received of the Lord's hand double for all her sins." According to the Orientalism the name of a man who was bankrupt was posted at the gate to the city by the Elders, along with the names of his creditors and how much he owed them. When the debts were completely paid, not partially paid, the Elders would double the paper over the man's name and nail it to the board. This signified that all which was against him was then blotted out, doubled. There was no longer condemnation against him. Christ our benefactor paid the debt in full, even when we were "dead in trespasses and sin." It is blotted out, for He "doubled" it for us. We received "double" for our sins because of Christ's payment for us.

> II Corinthians 5:21:
> For he [God] hath made him [Jesus] *to be* sin for us ... that we might be made the righteousness of God in him [that we might be made as righteous as God].

Isn't that wonderful! You ask, "Me, as righteous as God?" Yes, you.

Galatians 5:1:
Stand fast therefore in the liberty wherewith
Christ hath made us free ["Hath" is in the past
tense. How hath he made us free? By bearing that
cross, the cross of bondage, for us.], and be not
entangled again with the yoke of bondage.

Jesus bore that cross of bondage, the law, just for
you and for me that we need not live under that
bondage, "which neither our fathers nor we were able
to bear," according to Acts 15:10.

Not only was Jesus' cross composed of our transgressions and sins, plus the bondage of the law, but
also of our sicknesses.

Matthew 8:16,17:
When the even was come, they brought unto
him many that were possessed with devils: and
he cast out the spirits with *his* word, and healed
all that were sick [Jesus did this with His
Word]:

That it might be fulfilled which was spoken by
Esaias the prophet, saying, Himself took our
infirmities, and bare *our* sicknesses.

He became sickness just like He became sin. The
very last clause of Isaiah 53:5 says, "... and with his
stripes we are healed."

226

Isaiah 53:3—5:

He is despised and rejected of men; a man of
sorrows [pains], and acquainted with grief [sick-
ness]: and we hid as it were *our* faces from him;
he was despised, and we esteemed him not.

Surely he hath borne [carried or had put on
Him] our griefs [sicknesses], and carried our
sorrows [pains]: yet we did esteem him
stricken, smitten of God, and afflicted.

But he *was* wounded for our transgressions, *he
was* bruised for our iniquities: the chastisement
of our peace *was* upon him; and with his stripes
we are healed.

The cross of Jesus — what was it? John says they
"led *him* away. And he bearing his cross ...." The cross
Jesus bore was of sin, bondage, sickness and pain.

The unlearned man has made the cross of Jesus a
wooden cross. The Word says, and the spiritual man
knows, that Christ's cross was sin, bondage, sickness
and pain. A wooden cross could not accomplish anything, but the cross of Jesus did much.

I Corinthians 1:17,18:

For Christ sent me not to baptize, but to preach
the gospel: not with wisdom of words, lest the

cross of Christ should be made of none effect.

For the preaching of the cross [The wooden cross? No, the cross of Christ.] is to them that perish foolishness ....

Why does a millionaire act like a millionaire? Because he *believes* he has a million dollars. Does he have a million dollars laying in front of him? No! All he has is the broker's report that says he has so much in bonds and stocks; he has his banker's report and balance sheet indicating he has so much money in the bank; he has his attorney's record of his other properties. It is only *writing* — but he *believes* it. And, when he wants something, what does he do? He buys it. Why? Because He believes what is written. He believes the legal documents which indicate he is a millionaire.

The Bible is the legal document for us. This is our broker's report, the record of our bank account, our attorney's record. If a man of the world can walk by man's words, we as sons of God can walk by His Word. We must walk like it, talk like it, act like it. It does not matter what anyone else may say, I am and have what The Word says. Nothing that other people say can change what The Word says I am and I have. I believe what God says.

We must claim the promises of God like a business-man claims the benefits of what he has accomplished. Why not? "God is not a man that He should lie." The Word is as much God as God is Himself, just as your word is as much you as you are yourself. The Word of God is the Will of God. It means what it says and says what it means.

The devil and his corps of workers do not want us to understand that this cross of Christ took care of all our needs. No, the devil wants us to believe it was a wooden cross — something one gets splinters from, and then Satan beats us down with condemnation, sin, judgment, frustration, fear and defeat. The enemies of the cross of Christ are those who do not believe or accept what Jesus did. God says we are free because Christ bore all that is contrary to us, nailing it to *His* cross.

Stand fast, therefore, in the Lord. Jesus bore His cross — not of wood, but of sin and all its con-sequences — so that we could live the more abundant life. The wooden cross was borne by Simon of Cyrene; the spiritual cross, by Jesus.

When we consider the galaxies of personalities around the cross, of whom Simon was one, we un-cover a variety of men. The soldiers were there to see that the law was properly enforced and that the crucifixion went off according to schedule. The Jewish priests and rabbis, plus the majority of the members of the Jewish court of law, the Sanhedrin, were there to see that the Roman soldiers did their work properly and to see that this Jesus of Nazareth was put out of the way once and for all. A few of the disciples and close friends of Jesus were intermingled with the crowd to see their star of hope wane toward death; they loved Him as the Redeemer of Israel, but they had come to stand at a distance to see their last ray of hope pass on.

Most of the people gathered at the cross, however, were merely curiosity seekers. They had perhaps never heard of the condemned man before, but because so many people went to watch, they too followed. (Even today people flock to see a train wreck or an automobile accident.) Likewise these hordes of people followed the crowd. And yet, one man was at the foot of the cross who did not want to be there. Simon of Cyrene had no more desire to be at the crucifixion than you or I have to be present at the electrocution of a criminal. If you had told Simon on Tuesday that on the next day he would be an important character in the crucifixion of a "criminal," he would have laughed — but he was there.

Matthew, Mark and Luke each give us just one

verse about this man, which is all the information we have concerning him.

Matthew 27:32:
And as they came out, they found a man of Cyrene, Simon by name: him they compelled to bear his cross.

Mark 15:21:
And they compel one Simon a Cyrenian, who passed by, coming out of the country, the father of Alexander and Rufus, to bear his cross.

Luke 23:26:
And as they led him away, they laid hold upon one Simon, a Cyrenian, coming out of the country, and on him they laid the cross, that he might bear *it* after Jesus.

Yes, the man who did not want to be there, ended up being one of the central personalities around the cross: Simon, from the city of Cyrene. All he wanted was to be left alone — to be allowed to go his way. He was coming out of the country from the region beyond the gates; and, evidently, he was coming to Jerusalem to celebrate the Passover, when all at once his whole life took on a different perspective.

To this man, the bearing of the cross must have

231

been an extreme annoyance and indignity. He had business of his own to take care of. His family or his friends might have been waiting for him; but suddenly his own plans were dissolved. To touch the instrument of death, the cross, was as revolting to him as it would be for us to handle the hangman's rope or to press the button in the electrocution chamber — perhaps more so, because it was Passover time and this act would make him ceremonially unclean. Had Simon entered the city one hour sooner or one hour later, his life's history might have been entirely different.

Sometimes when we want to be alone, when we don't want to be interfered with, it is just then that an interference may make all the difference in the world; the greatest change may hinge on the smallest circumstances. To Simon, this encounter undoubtedly seemed at the moment the most unfortunate incident that could have befallen him — an interruption, an annoyance and a humiliation — yet it turned out to be the gateway of life.

Are you spiritually in the condition that you just want to be left alone? The interruption of Christ into your life right now will make all the difference in the world for you, for your children and for your children's children. It made a great difference for Simon.

"Simon a Cyrenian ... the father of Alexander and Rufus." Evidently the two sons of Simon were well-known to those to whom Mark was writing. Compelling Simon to bear the cross may have resulted in his salvation and in the salvation of his house. Let me ask you this question and then be honest with yourself: Are you the kind of parent that your children can be proud of? Will they twenty-five years from now, remember you because of the heritage you extended to them? Are you setting a good example for your children? Are you leading your children to Christ or away from Him? The Bible says, "So then every one of us shall give account of himself to God." Some day you and I as parents must give an account of our lives. Do we instruct them in what we would like to have them do, and then do we continue to live in a haphazard way? Look at your child this moment, are you a real parent to him? Are you a Christian?

The Apostle Paul tells us of our ultimate responsibility.

Ephesians 4:1:
I ... beseech you that ye walk worthy of the vocation wherewith ye are called.

Our Christian vocation is a responsibility of pure delight. Our joyous cross is to live to carry forth the good news of His accomplishments. Jesus Christ suf-

233

fered and died so that we can live with power.

We are inclined to speak of trouble as a kind of cross. But properly speaking, Christ bore the real cross on our behalf. The scorn, loss and censure is the cross Christ bore that we might have joy in speaking to another in Christ's name. The time we give in Christian work, the giving of our means that the gospel of Christ may be spread at home and abroad, and manifesting the power of God in our lives — yes, this is the living, joyous cross *we* bear.

The Four Crucified With Jesus

In the Word of God, we are instructed to divide the Word of God rightly, which means that it must be accurately divided.* The major reason for so much confusion regarding the "others" crucified with Jesus is that men have divided the Word of God to suit themselves and according to tradition. We have failed to give sufficient heed to The Word and to rightly dividing it. We must change our theology and beliefs to agree with The Word.

Before we proceed to read accurately and to study what is written, allow me to indicate to you the problems created by traditional teaching. The two thieves and the two malefactors have by tradition been made the same. In other words, only two were crucified with Jesus. If this were true, we would have a major discrepancy in the Word of God. Matthew

*II Timothy 2:15: "Study to shew thyself approved unto God, a workman that needeth not to be ashamed, rightly dividing the word of truth."

27:38 and Mark 15:27 distinctly state that there were "two thieves" while Luke 23:32 says "two malefactors."

Furthermore, *both* thieves (or robbers) reviled Jesus according to Matthew 27:44 and Mark 15:32, while in Luke 23:39 and 40 only *one* of the malefactors "railed on him [Jesus]" while the other malefactor defended Jesus.

Another added discrepancy by tradition is regarding the two malefactors who were "led with him to be put to death" according to Luke 23. And when they had arrived at Calvary they, then and there, "crucified him, and the malefactors, one on the right hand and the other on the left." Yet, Matthew 27 says that after a number of things had already happened at Calvary, "Then were there two thieves [robbers] crucified with him."

If all of this is synonymous and dealing with two individuals only, then language is useless for communication purposes. The Bible then is just another book written by men engrossed in frailties and errors, and not what The Word says of itself in II Peter 1:21, namely, "... holy men of God spake *as they were* moved by the Holy Ghost."

The following are a few Greek words employed in the part of the Word of God we are going to consider. These words are critical to preface a minute study of each record.

duo lēstai means "two robbers" — not thieves

duo kakourgoi means "two malefactors"

allos means "the 'other' or second of two when and where there may be more."

heteros means "the 'other' or second of two when and where there are *only* two."

Regarding this subject of the five crosses,* we want to note first of all Matthew 27.

Matthew 27:35-38:
And they crucified him, and parted his garments, casting lots: that it might be fulfilled which was spoken by the prophet, They parted my garments among them, and upon my vesture did they cast lots.

*At Ploubezere near Lannion, in the Cotes-du-Nord, Brittany, there is a representation of Calvary with five crosses. According to the Encyclopedia Brittanica the "altar slab" when consecrated in a Roman Catholic Church has cut in it five crosses: one cross is in the center and one cross is in each of the four corners. This may be a practice in line with the "other four" crucified with Jesus.

And sitting down they watched him there;

And set up over his head his accusation written, THIS IS JESUS THE KING OF THE JEWS.

Then were there two thieves [*duo lēstai*] crucified with him, one on the right hand, and another on the left.

The King James says "two thieves;" the Greek words are *duo lēstai* of which *duo* is two, *lēstai* is robbers. The Greeks used an entirely different word for thieves, *kleptēs*.* A thief is one who acts stealthily while a robber is one who deliberately plans and openly carries out his dirty work, using violence if necessary. In legal terms robbery is a worse crime than thievery. Thieves would be punished, but not by such an extreme sentence as crucifixion. Robbers would receive a crucifixion sentence because of more extreme actions. This distinction is obscured in the King James Version. *Duo lēstai,* two robbers, were crucified with Jesus after an interim of time.

The Word of God says plainly that the soldiers crucified Jesus, they parted His garments, sat down and "then [then] were there two thieves [*duo lēstai*] crucified with him ...."

*The English word "kleptomaniac" comes from this Greek word *kleptēs.* Violence is not usually associated with a kleptomaniac.

Verse 44:
The thieves [*duo lēstai*] also, which were crucified with him, cast the same in his teeth.

As the bystanders mocked Jesus, the robbers, two
of them, not just one, joined in with the crowd.

Mark 15 contains the second account of the crucifixion.

Mark 15:24-27:
And when they had crucified him, they parted
his garments, casting lots upon them, what every
man should take.

And it was the third hour, and they crucified
him.

And the superscription of his accusation was
written over, THE KING OF THE JEWS.

And with him they crucify two thieves [*duo
lēstai*]; the one on his right hand, and the other
on his left.

The two robbers (*duo lēstai*) were crucified *after*
the garments were parted. After Jesus had been nailed
on the cross, the crowd reproached Jesus.

239

Verse 32:
Let Christ the King of Israel descend now from the cross, that we may see and believe. And they [*duo lēstai*, verse 27] that were crucified with him reviled him.

The Gospels of Matthew and Mark tell about the robbers not the malefactors.

Luke 23:32:
And there were also two other, malefactors [*duo kakourgoi*], led with him to be put to death.

Luke says there were two malefactors (*duo kakourgoi*) led with Jesus when He was led forth to be put to death. Matthew and Mark concur that there were two robbers (*duo lēstai*) crucified with Him *after* the garments had been parted and the soldiers had sat down and were watching what was going on.

The two malefactors (*duo kakourgoi*) were crucified at the time Jesus was crucified, while the two robbers (*duo lēstai*) were crucified later. The malefactors (*duo kakourgoi*) were led *with* Him from Pilate's Hall and crucified at the time Jesus was crucified.

Luke 23:32,33:
And there were also two other, malefactors [*duo*

kakourgoi], led with him to be put to death.

And when they were come to the place, which is called Calvary, there they crucified him, and the malefactors, one on the right hand, and the other on the left.

The two malefactors were then on either side next to our Lord Jesus Christ.

Luke 23:39:
And one of the malefactors [not both] which were hanged railed on him, saying, If thou be Christ, save thyself and us.

Luke says that *one* malefactor railed on Him.

Luke 23:40-43:
But the other [the other malefactor] answering rebuked him [the malefactor], saying, Dost not thou fear God, seeing thou art in the same condemnation?

And we indeed justly; for we receive the due reward of our deeds: but this man hath done nothing amiss.

And he said unto Jesus, Lord, remember me when thou comest into thy kingdom.

241

And Jesus said unto him, Verily I say unto thee, To day shalt thou be with me in paradise [The comma should be after "To day." Paradise is still future.].

Matthew as well as Mark records that the robbers both reviled Christ. The Gospel of Luke has only one reviling Christ and that one is called a malefactor. In Matthew and Mark the two robbers were not crucified until *after* Christ's garments had been divided. In Luke two malefactors were led forth with Christ from the presence of Pilate and were crucified at the same time as Jesus Christ.

There is a simple answer to understanding the Word of God: just believe what is written. Instead of being conditioned by the pictures we have seen, we must believe what The Word says. Two malefactors were crucified with Jesus at the time He was crucified, and two robbers were crucified with Him after the garments were parted. Of the two malefactors, one was on His right and the other was on His left; and also of the two robbers, one was on His right and the other on His left. So the answer to this subject is simple. Four were crucified with Jesus.

Every robber is a malefactor (evil-doer), but not every malefactor (evil-doer) is a robber. If I break a law, I am not necessarily a robber; but I am a male-

242

factor. The Word of God does not tell what the two malefactors did to deserve crucifixion.

The Gospel of John is not concerned about the time element. It does not give the *when*, but it gives the *where*. John culminates this whole subject.

John 19:17,18:
And he bearing his cross went forth into a place called *the place* of a skull, which is called in the Hebrew Golgotha:

Where they crucified him, and two other with him, on either side one, and Jesus in the midst.

One small word from John 19:18 should immediately attract our attention, and that is the word "midst." It means *middle*. The word "midst" is a key word because grammatically one individual cannot be crucified in the *midst* of two. With the use of the word "midst" four, six or eight are indicated. When a person is situated with one on either side, the person is not in the midst; he is *between*. A person is between two, but in the midst of four.

An interlinear translation of the Stephens Greek Text, from which the King James was translated, reads in John 19:18, "and with him, others two on this side and on that side." The word "one" appears in the English, but no corresponding Greek word is above it. To indicate that the translators added the word "one" they put it in brackets. The King James translators, therefore, added the word "one." If the word "one" is not in the critical Greek texts, why is it in the King James? Because by 1611 the Western world had been so indoctrinated by a picture showing Jesus on the center cross and one evil-doer on either side of Him that, when the translators were translating this particular verse of the nineteenth chapter of John, they inserted the word "one."

> John 19:32,33:
> Then came the soldiers, and brake the legs of the first, and of the other which was crucified with him.
>
> But when they came to Jesus, and saw that he was dead already, they brake not his legs.

To illustrate how we have been taught about the way the soldiers went about breaking the legs of the miscalled two thieves: the soldiers broke the legs of the first; then they must have bypassed Jesus and gone around Him to the second miscalled thief; and finally these soldiers came back to Jesus and said, 'My goodness, He's dead already." This type of routine isn't very logical. As a matter of fact, it is senseless.

When you read the accuracy of The Word, the soldiers came and they broke the legs of the first and of the other. Progressing in the row, the soldiers came to Jesus in the third place and they found Him already dead. When Jesus was crucified, the two malefactors were next to Him, one on each side, and the robbers were one removed from Jesus, one on each side. So the soldiers came; they broke the legs of the first, the robber, and of the next, the malefactor, and then Jesus was next in line: "And coming to Jesus they found that he was dead already." Then it fits like a hand in a glove and you don't have to close your eyes and run around Jesus and sound foolish and illogical.

Listen again to John 19, "Then came the soldiers, and brake the legs of the first [a robber], and of the other [a malefactor] which was crucified with him." The word "with" in this verse does not indicate the same time. It is the Greek word *sun*, meaning "in close proximity with." The word "him" refers back to the word "first," a robber. The malefactor was crucified in close proximity with a robber.

The word "other" in verse 32 — "and of the other

which was crucified with him" — is another key to add to the proof that four men were crucified with Jesus. There are two words that are translated "other" in the Bible. One word is the word *heteros,* and the other Greek word is *allos.* These words make all the difference between truth and error. Both *heteros* and *allos* are translated "other" but their usage is for two different situations. The word "other" in John 19:32 is *allos.* The word *allos* is used when more than two may be involved. The two malefactors and the two thieves (robbers) make four. So the soldiers broke the legs of the first and of the other (*allos*) of the four involved. That is why they use the word *allos* for the word "other."

In Luke 23:32 the English word "other" was also used.

> Luke 23:32:
> And there were also two other, malefactors, led
> with him ....

The word for "other" here is not the word *allos,* but it is *heteros* because there were only two involved, two malefactors. This is the unbelievable accuracy of God's Word. They led the two malefactors with Him; later, after they had crucified Jesus, they parted His garments, they cast lots, they sat down, they put up an accusation, then finally they brought the two robbers and they crucified them. Two plus two make four. When the soldiers came, they broke the legs of the first and of the other (the *allos*, of more than two), but having come to Jesus they found that He was dead already. Why? Because the prophets of old had prophesied that no one would ever break the Messiah's legs.* The Jews and the soldiers didn't take Jesus' life upon Calvary's cross; He laid it down, He gave up His life. He didn't die because they crucified Him, He died because He gave Himself for you and for me. This is the accuracy with which the Word of God fits and this is the remarkable usage of The Word as it develops the Scriptures by interpreting itself right where it is written.

*Psalms 34:20: "He keepeth all his bones: not one of them is broken."
Exodus 12:46: "In one house shall it be eaten; thou shalt not carry forth ought of the flesh abroad out of the house; neither shall ye break a bone thereof."
Numbers 9:12: "They shall leave none of it unto the morning, nor break any bone of it: according to all the ordinances of the passover they shall keep it."

CHAPTER SIXTEEN

The Burial of Jesus

In studying the burial of Jesus, we will look at the records given in each of the four Gospels. These four Scriptural passages, in complementing each other's reports, give a total view of the interesting and involved proceedings in the burial of Jesus. Joseph of Arimathea and Nicodemus are the two active participants in burying Jesus. Except for Jesus' burial, Joseph of Arimathea is mentioned in no other Biblical record and Nicodemus is mentioned in only two other places, John 3 and John 7. As we shall see, each man worked independently of the other, one with the idea that Jesus was temporarily dead and the other believing that Jesus was truly to remain perpetually in His lifeless condition. Mary Magdalene and "the other Mary" also tried to participate in the burial customs for their dead Master, but they were too late to do so in arriving at the empty tomb early on Sunday morning.

It is important to keep in mind that no single Gospel gives the entire picture of the burial of Jesus. For example, what John tells in his account is not identical to what Matthew, Mark and Luke tell; yet there is no contradiction among them when the Word of God is rightly divided, noting carefully time and place of action and who is involved.

Let us study the burial of Jesus by going through the Gospels beginning in Matthew.

> Matthew 27:57:
> When the even was come, there came a rich man of Arimathaea, named Joseph, who also himself was Jesus' disciple.

There are two "evens" referred to in the Scriptures. One "even" is from three o'clock in the afternoon until sundown; the other "even" is after sundown. This "even" of Matthew 27:57 is between 3 P.M. and sunset for we know from the Biblical record in Matthew 27:46, as well as the other Gospels, that Jesus died at the ninth hour which corresponds to three o'clock in the afternoon as we reckon time.

The words "a rich man" show that Joseph was abounding in riches. He was a very wealthy man who lived in Arimathea, approximately twenty-five miles from Jerusalem. Being "Jesus' disciple" means that he

250

was technically discipled to Jesus, a pupil of Jesus, a student, convinced because of his own searching.

Verse 58:
He [Joseph of Arimathaea] went to Pilate, and begged the body of Jesus. Then Pilate commanded the body to be delivered.

Remember that Joseph was a Jew and Pilate a Gentile. Entering into the court of a Gentile to request the body of Jesus made Joseph ceremonially unclean to eat the Passover. For this reason, the rulers of the synagogue would not enter Pilate's judgment hall when Jesus was led in earlier that day.

John 18:28
Then led they Jesus from Caiaphas unto the hall of judgment: and it was early; and they themselves [these rulers, scribes and Pharisees] went not into the judgment hall, lest they should be defiled; but that they might eat the passover.

Joseph earnestly appealed to Pilate to give him Jesus' body. Certainly, under normal circumstances, no person would beg for a criminal's body; in fact if a person had a dead criminal's body, he would try to get rid of it as soon as possible, preferably without touching it. Yet Joseph went to Pilate's hall begging, "Please, Pilate, let me have the body of Jesus." How

Joseph must have loved Him.

> Matthew 27:59:
> And when Joseph had taken the body, he wrapped it [the body] in a clean linen cloth.

Notice that nothing is said about Nicodemus' aiding Joseph in any way. It was Joseph of Arimathea who, after Pilate commanded the body to be delivered, took the body of Jesus and wrapped it in a clean cloth. The words "wrapped it" mean "rolled it up in." This does not mean that he "wound" his trunk, head and limbs in a burial fashion. The word for "linen cloth" is the Greek word *sindōn*. This clean "linen cloth" was not the regular grave wrapping, for which an entirely different word is used. The linen cloth which Joseph wrapped around the body of Jesus was a sheet of material which could be wrapped around any body, not necessarily a dead body. The same word *sindōn* is used again in Mark 14:51 as we shall see later.

> Verse 60:
> And laid it in his own new tomb [sepulchre], which he had hewn out in the rock: and he rolled a great stone to the door of the sepulchre, and departed.

A question which this verse arouses is why should

Joseph of Arimathea have a tomb or a sepulchre in Jerusalem right next to the place where criminals were executed? This just doesn't make sense unless we realize that this particular sepulchre was a memorial specifically prepared by Joseph of Arimathea at this accessible location that it might be the burying place or tomb for Jesus.

The word for "had hewn" in verse 60, in contrast to "had taken" in verse 59, is in the passive voice in the Aramaic text, indicating that Joseph previously had the memorial hewn out by someone else; he himself did not hew it out. Verse 60 then notes that Joseph rolled the "great stone" to the door of the sepulchre and departed. Notice that there was no anointing, there were no spices used, there were no wrappings of grave clothes.

> Verse 61:
> And there was Mary Magdalene, and the other Mary, sitting over against the sepulchre [*taphos*].

The word "against" means "on the opposite side of, away from, in front of, or facing," just as though one would be sitting in front of a fireplace.

Joseph had his men hew out of the rock a tomb which being a memorial was also referred to as a sepulchre. According to Biblical usage a sepulchre may be a tomb but a tomb is not necessarily a sepulchre. The word for "sepulchre" in verse 60 is *mnēmeion* meaning "monument;" while the word for "tomb" in verse 61 is *taphos* meaning "a place where one is buried."

The women who were present observed everything that was done by Joseph of Arimathea and, of course, they noted that Joseph did not properly bury Jesus according to Jewish custom. Why did Joseph not anoint Him with spices and wrap Him in the burial clothing? All the actions of Joseph of Arimathea indicate that burial rites were unnecessary, for he believed that Jesus Christ would rise again. The word "disciple" discussed earlier, does not mean that he was simply a casual pupil or student of Jesus, but that he was a convinced follower who believed literally the words of Jesus. Specifically regarding the apostles and the other disciples, John 20:9 says, "For as yet they knew not the scripture, that he must rise again from the dead." From context, the word "they" in this Scripture could not be referring to Joseph of Arimathea.

After the Matthew 27 account, the next record in the Bible regarding the burial of Jesus is found in Mark 15:42-47.

254

Mark 15:42:
And now when the even was come, because it was the preparation, that is, the day before the sabbath.

The word "even" is the same word used in Matthew 27:57, meaning the period of time between three o'clock in the afternoon and sunset.

This verse directly informs us that the day Jesus Christ died was the fourteenth of Nisan, the day before the Passover. Passover was always a Sabbath, the "high day" of John 19:31 and not the regular weekly Sabbath.

Verse 43:
Joseph of Arimathaea, an honourable counseller, which also waited for the kingdom of God, came, and went in boldly unto Pilate, and craved the body of Jesus.

This record tells us a little more about Joseph; namely, that he was "an honourable counseller," that is, he was a member of the Council, the Sanhedrin, the ruling body of the Jews in Jerusalem. He was also waiting for the Kingdom of God.

The word "craved" in verse 43 is the same word "begged" used in Matthew 27:58.

Verse 44:

And Pilate marvelled [questioned with surprise] if he [Jesus] were already dead: and calling *unto him* the centurion, he asked him whether he had been any while dead.

Pilate was not convinced by the word of Joseph so he asked the centurion if Jesus were truly dead. I am deeply impressed with the boldness of Joseph of Arimathea in every record. Mark 14:50 says regarding the apostles, "And they all forsook him, and fled." Yet Joseph was bold. He was not one of the twelve disciples, but he was one who believed Jesus. The apostles may have been closely associated with Jesus during His earthly life, but under the adversity of this critical time, they fled. Yet Joseph, instead of cowering, acted with conviction.

Verse 45:

And when he [Pilate] knew *it* [that Jesus was dead] of the centurion, he gave the body to Joseph.

Verse 46:

And he [Joseph] bought fine linen, and took him down, and wrapped him in the linen, and laid him in a sepulchre which was hewn out of a rock, and rolled a stone unto the door of the sepulchre.

256

Note that Joseph "bought," deliberately purchased for this person who was very special to him, a new wrapping or sheet which here again is called "fine linen," the same word as used in Matthew, *sindōn*. Also this verse specifically states that he (Joseph) took Jesus down from the cross. The word for "wrapped him" is again the same word as "rolled him up in" regular linen material; he did not put the body in grave clothes.

Verse 47:
And Mary Magdalene and Mary *the mother* of Joses beheld where he was laid.

Once more there is no mention whatsoever in this Gospel of the presence of Nicodemus although Mark again states that the women stayed around and watched Joseph of Arimathea as he was burying Jesus. There was no anointing with oil and spices for burial according to the proper method of a Jewish burial.

The next record regarding Joseph's ministering to the dead body of Jesus is in Luke 23:50–56.

Luke 23:50:
And, behold, *there was* a man named Joseph, a counseller; *and he was* a good man, and a just.

257

The word "good" used here means that he was worthy to be admired, a person to be looked up to.

> Verse 51:
> (The same had not consented to the counsel and deed of them;) *he was* of Arimathaea, a city of the Jews: who also himself waited for the kingdom of God.

This verse in Luke gives more information regarding Joseph than does Matthew or Mark. It tells that he was not only a member of the Council, the Sanhedrin, but that he did not consent to the majority rule and the deeds carried out by that Council.

> Verse 52:
> This *man* went unto Pilate, and begged the body of Jesus.

> Verse 53:
> And he took it down, and wrapped it in linen, and laid it in a sepulchre that was hewn in stone, wherein never man before was laid.

Luke gives the same description as in the two other Gospels with the word *sindōn*, "wrapped it in linen."

> Verse 54:
> And that day was the preparation, and the sabbath drew on.

The day once more is noted as the day of preparation, the fourteenth of Nisan.

Verse 55:
And the women also, which came after him from Galilee, followed after, and beheld the sepulchre, and how his body was laid.

These women can be identified from Mark 15:40 and 41 which read, "There were also women looking on afar off: among whom was Mary Magdalene, and Mary the mother of James the less and of Joses, and Salome; (Who also, when he was in Galilee, followed him, and ministered unto him;) and many other women which came up with him unto Jerusalem."

These women came from Galilee and beheld the sepulchre and "how his body was laid." In other words, they observed exactly what Joseph of Arimathea had done. He simply wrapped Jesus in a *sindōn* but did not properly anoint His body with spices and oils according to Jewish burial customs nor wind his body in burial cloths. Because the women saw that Joseph of Arimathea did not give Jesus' body the proper rites, they took the ritual into their own hands.

Verse 56:
And they [the women] returned [to

Jerusalem], and prepared spices and ointments; and rested the sabbath day [both the high day, Passover and the weekly sabbath] according to the commandment.

Matthew, Mark and Luke concur that it was Joseph of Arimathea who took the body of Jesus down from the cross after Pilate had given him permission to do so. He wrapped Jesus' body in a linen cloth, a *sindōn,* and laid it in his own sepulchre without giving Jesus the traditional Jewish burial procedure.

Reading John 19:38–42, we find some interesting added truths which do not contradict but which enlarge upon that which the other three Gospels have told.

John 19:38:
And after this Joseph of Arimathaea, being a disciple of Jesus, but secretly for fear of the Jews, besought Pilate that he might take away the body of Jesus: and Pilate gave *him* leave. He came therefore, and took the body of Jesus.

"And after this" refers to the soldiers coming to break the legs of Jesus.

"And after this Joseph of Arimathaea, being a disciple of Jesus" is the same information as recorded

260

by the other three writers; but then comes a statement which the other Gospels did not tell, namely, "but secretly for fear of the Jews." The word "secretly" would lead one to think that Joseph was afraid of what would happen to him if the Jews found out about his activities. This is certainly a contradictory idea about Joseph compared to his boldness as posited in the other passages. To clarify the apparent problem, the word translated "secretly" is the verb *kruptō* in the Greek text. Therefore the verse should read, "After this Joseph of Arimathea being a convinced follower, an earnest student or disciple of Jesus, but hidden away for fear of the Jews." He was hidden away, crypted, during the crucifixion events. So to fit Mark 15:43, when Joseph came boldly to Pilate to ask for the body of Jesus, with John 19:38, when Joseph hid away for fear of the Jews, we should note that Joseph of Arimathea apparently was not afraid of what might happen to him eventually; but he was concealed for the duration of the crucifixion because he wanted to be sure not only to be able to see what was going on, but to be alive and boldly claim the body of Jesus upon death. Joseph obviously believed that Jesus was going to die and therefore bought a garden near to the place of the crucifixion in which he had a sepulchre hewn out of the rock. Certainly Joseph would never have done this had he not believed what Jesus told him concerning His death.

261

Verse 39:
And there came also Nicodemus, which at the
first came to Jesus by night, and brought a
mixture of myrrh and aloes, about an hundred
pound *weight*.

Until this verse Nicodemus has not been mentioned
in the Gospel records. The added note "And there
came also Nicodemus, which at the first came to
Jesus by night ..." identifies Nicodemus as being the
same man as told of in John 3 and John 7. The first
mention of spices in any of the Gospels is when
Nicodemus came and "brought a mixture of myrrh
and aloes" for the proper burial of Jesus.

Verse 40:
Then took they the body of Jesus, and wound it
in linen clothes with the spices, as the manner of
the Jews is to bury.

The word "they" in the King James has left the
impression that it was Joseph of Arimathea and
Nicodemus, but this cannot be true from the records
given in the other three Gospels. In the Aramaic text
the word "they" is the word "he." If the word were
"they," "they" would have to refer to Nicodemus
and his helpers, excluding Joseph of Arimathea.

Verse 40 is the first time the word "wound" is

used. In the other Gospels Joseph *wrapped* the body of Jesus in a *sindōn*. In this verse Nicodemus *wound* the body of Jesus with the spices in linen clothes. Here the Greek word for "linen clothes" is *othonion* meaning "bandages or wrappings, grave clothes." These are striking truths.

According to John 20:5, John the Apostle on the first day of the week came to the sepulchre and "stooping down ... saw the linen clothes ...." In verse 6 Simon Peter entered in the sepulchre and he "seeth the linen clothes lie ...." The word for "linen clothes" in both verses is not *sindōn*, but *othonion*, meaning "wrapping."

> Verse 41:
> Now in the place where he was crucified there was a garden; and in the garden a new sepulchre, wherein was never man yet laid.

This is the same garden where the women saw Joseph of Arimathea place the body of Jesus and where Mary Magdalene met Jesus after His resurrection.

> Verse 42:
> There laid they ["he," the same as in verse 40] Jesus therefore [after Nicodemus had properly anointed the body and wrapped it for Jewish

263

burial] because of the Jews' preparation *day*
[because the Sabbath was approaching]; for the
sepulchre was nigh at hand.

"Because" is the Greek word *dia*. This word indicates that Nicodemus laid Jesus back in this sepulchre
because time was running out before the Jewish Passover began, which, of course, would occur at sunset.
This verse well-documents the fact that sunset was
near when Nicodemus came to properly anoint the
body.

Putting all the truths together from the four
Gospels, we note that Joseph of Arimathea, after
receiving permission from Pilate, took the body of
Jesus, rolled it in a *sindōn*, put it in his own sepulchre
which he had prepared for the occasion, rolled the
stone to the door of the sepulchre and departed. The
women who had been sitting a short distance from
the sepulchre noted Joseph's treatment of Jesus'
body as he placed Him in this tomb and returned to
Jerusalem to prepare the spices and ointment for
proper burial without any knowledge of what Nicodemus would do. Nicodemus, after Joseph of
Arimathea had departed from the garden, came to
the sepulchre and properly wrapped the body in grave

clothes with spices and buried Jesus according to the Jewish custom.

The total picture, drawn by studying collectively these four accounts, is most interesting. The human elements as shown by Joseph and Nicodemus make us think of our own experience. We do not always think someone else's work is adequate so we re-do it to meet our satisfaction or approval. Sometimes the situation is not clearly understood, similar to Nicodemus' not expecting the less-than-seventy-two-hour-away resurrection of Jesus Christ. Thus he did unnecessary work in anointing and wrapping in grave clothes the dead body. In contrast to all the others, Joseph of Arimathea seemed unique in that he was the *only* person prepared for the crucifixion and resurrection of Jesus. He had bought a location in a garden near Golgotha and had a sepulchre hewn out. After receiving permission to take the body of Jesus, Joseph of Arimathea gave it tender though minimal care. Joseph's actions confirmed that he believed the Lord's teaching that He would rise three days and three nights after being buried.

Perhaps someone will now ask you as I have been asked hundreds of times, "What difference does it make if Joseph of Arimathea and Nicodemus worked independently of each other?" It makes all the difference between an unerring, accurate Word and a crumbling jumble of writing. If God thought it important enough to sacrifice His only-begotten Son for the integrity of His Word, then we ought to think it supremely important to accurately divide that Word.

The Cry of Triumph

Jesus' cry of triumph, one of the last statements Jesus made while hanging on the cross just before giving up His life, is recorded in Matthew.

Matthew 27:46:
And about the ninth hour Jesus cried with a loud voice, saying, Eli, Eli, lama sabachthani? that is to say, My God, my God, why hast thou forsaken me?

Does this sound like a cry of triumph — "My God, my God, why hast thou forsaken me?" Certainly not, not as the English translation now sets. This translation is a cry of defeat and as such has misled well-meaning people for years.

We understand Matthew 27:46 word by word except for the foreign words. It would appear that God forsook Jesus because Jesus became sin and God could not stand sin. God consequently left Jesus to die alone. This idea contradicts every other pertinent verse in the Word of God.

Matthew 27:46, as well as the same record in Mark 15:34, should have arrested our attention from the beginning. Why did the translators leave those foreign words in the verse? This deviation from normal translation procedures should have caused us to wonder.

Let us go to The Word and see exactly what The Word says. Look at the Gospel of John where Jesus spoke to His apostles.

> John 16:32:
> Behold, the hour cometh, yea, is now come, that ye shall be scattered, every man to his own, and shall leave me alone: and yet I am not alone, because the Father is with me.

Jesus was referring to the time of His crucifixion and of His death, the coming time; He said, "the Father is with me." Yet Matthew 27:46 says, "My God, my God why hast thou forsaken me?"

John 10:30 testifies, "I and *my* Father are one." II Corinthians 5:19 says, "To wit, that God was in Christ, reconciling the world unto himself." How are you going to separate one, separate God who was in

Christ, when He was dying on the cross?

Colossians 2:9 tells, "For in him [in Christ] dwelleth all the fulness of the Godhead bodily." How are we going to separate the fullness of the Godhead which dwelt in Christ while He was present on earth? How was it possible for God to forsake Jesus when Jesus was the fullness of the Godhead?

Matthew tells what Jesus said at the time He was taken captive.

> Matthew 26:53:
> Thinkest thou that I cannot now pray to my Father, and he shall presently give me more than twelve legions of angels?

A person has to be on talking terms with God to get that kind of assistance. The Father would have given Jesus 72,000 angels. Jesus could have walked right out from among this group of men if He had wanted to. How? Because "I and *my* Father are one," "the Father is with me," "I always do the Father's will." If Jesus Christ was *always* doing the Father's will, He must have been doing His Father's will when He was dying upon the cross. Yet Matthew 27:46 says, "Jesus cried with a loud voice, saying, Eli, Eli, lama sabachthani? that is to say, My God, my God, why hast thou forsaken me?" This verse clearly contradicts the rest of The Word.

What is the problem? First of all, the foreign words in verse 46 of Matthew 27 are not Greek words; they are Aramaic. Jesus spoke Aramaic. (Aramaic is called Hebrew in the King James Version.) These Aramaic words show up in this particular Scripture because the translators were not absolutely certain about their meaning. They let the Aramaic words remain and then, also, added what they thought the English translation might be.* However, there is no such Aramaic word as *lama,* but there is the word *lmna.* *Lmna* is a declaration of "for this purpose" or "for this reason." The root of *sabachthani* is *shbk* or *shbq.* The root word *shbk* means to spare, to leave, to reserve or to keep. The word "reserved" in Romans 11:4 is the root word *shbk* which must have been the same word in the ancient text of I Kings 19:18 from which it is quoted.

> Romans 11:4:
> But what saith the answer of God unto him? I have reserved [*shbk*] to myself seven thousand men, who have not bowed the knee to *the image of* Baal.

*There are a few other examples in the New Testament to this day where the translators have allowed the Aramaic words to remain: Matthew 5:22; Mark 5:41; I Corinthians 16:22.

I Kings 19:18:
Yet I have left *me* seven thousand in Israel, all the knees which have not bowed unto Baal, and every mouth which hath not kissed him.

This same *shbk* is translated "remaining" in the following three Scriptures.

II Kings 10:11:
So Jehu slew all that remained of the house of Ahab in Jezreel, and all his great men, and his kinsfolks, and his priests, until he left him none remaining [*shbk*].

Deuteronomy 3:3:
So the Lord our God delivered into our hands Og also, the king of Bashan, and all his people: and we smote him until none was left to him remaining [*shbk*].

Joshua 10:33:
Then Horam king of Gezer came up to help Lachish; and Joshua smote him and his people, until he had left him none remaining [*shbk*].

Going back to Matthew 27, it was about the ninth hour, three o'clock in the afternoon, when Jesus spoke from the cross. Hanging on the cross at that critical hour, Jesus came forth with this utterance from the depth of His soul, "My God, my God [*Eli, Eli*], for this purpose [*lmna*] you spared me [*sabachthani*]." "My God, my God, for this purpose was I spared or reserved."

The next words that He uttered were, "It is finished." What was finished? Your redemption and mine. Jesus Christ had given His own life and paid the price. He who knew no sin had become sin so that you and I might become the righteousness of God in Him.* Your redemption and mine was finished then. The next chronological verse of Scripture says, "and he ... yielded up the ghost." The soldiers and accusers did not take His life. It was not the nails driven through His hands that held Him to the cross, not the nails driven through His feet. Do you know why Jesus kept hanging on that cross? Because Jesus Christ loved us. He could have walked off that cross; He could have had twelve legions of angels at His command; but He kept hanging on the cross because He so loved us that He gave His own life for us. And under these circumstances, do you think God would desert His only Son?

Suppose you had an only son and right now your son was dying. Would you be reading this book on abundant living or would you be with your son? And

*II Corinthians 5:21: "For he hath made him *to be* sin for us, who knew no sin; that we might be made the righteousness of God in him."

yet your son has sinned; he has done things contrary to what you would like for him to do. Still you would want to be with him. Do you think that God Almighty is less caring for His Son than you are? Jesus Christ was God's only-begotten Son; Jesus always did the Father's will. When He was dying upon the cross, where do you think the Father was? With Him!

When Jesus was dying upon the cross, He did *not* cry, "My God, my God, why hast thou forsaken me," but rather, "My God, my God, for this purpose was I spared, for this purpose was I kept, for this purpose came I into the world, for this purpose was I reserved.* Now we have an accurate translation of Matthew 27:46, one of the most difficult verses of Scripture in the King James Version. Now this verse harmonizes or fits with the other passages in the Word of God.

God stayed with His Son. This was not only *their* triumphant hour but *ours* also, for it was at this point that Jesus Christ, the second Adam, fulfilled all the legal requirements for our redemption and salvation. This was Christ's purpose for coming into the world.

---

*Translations from the East read in Matthew 27:46, "My God, my God, for this purpose was I spared." The Occidental or Western translations erroneously read, "My God, my God, why hast thou forsaken me?"

About the Author

Victor Paul Wierwille has spent many years searching, and seeking enlightenment on God's Word from men of God scattered across the continent. His academic career after high school continued at the Mission House (Lakeland) College and Seminary, Sheboygan, Wisconsin, where he received his Bachelor of Arts and Bachelor of Divinity degrees. Dr. Wierwille studied at the University of Chicago and at Princeton Theological Seminary where he was awarded the Master of Theology degree in Practical Theology. Later he completed his work for the Doctor of Theology degree.

For sixteen years Dr. Wierwille served as a pastor in northwestern Ohio. During these years he searched the Word of God for keys to powerful victorious living. Dr. Wierwille visited E. Stanley Jones and studied his Ashram program. Such men as Glenn Clark, Rufus Mosley, Starr Daily, Albert Cliffe, Bishop K.C. Pillai and others were guests of Dr. Wierwille's local congregation. Karl Barth of Switzerland was a friend and consultant, as is George M. Lamsa, the Aramaic scholar, as well as other European and Far Eastern scholars. With these men Dr. Wierwille quested for Biblical enlightenment. In 1953 he began teaching classes on Power for Abundant Living. These concentrated sessions are specifically directed to unfold the Word of God as the Will of God and to answer crucial questions regarding the holy spirit and its present availability and efficacy in believers' lives. Leading men and women from all over the world into receiving the more abundant life quickly consumed Dr. Wierwille's full time, so it became necessary for him to resign his local pastorate. Since that time Dr. Wierwille has devoted his entire energy to The Way Biblical Research Center in New Knoxville, Ohio. There, as elsewhere in the United States and foreign countries, he continues to study, write and teach the greatness of God's Word.

276